The First-Mate's Guide to Cruising the Inside Passage

The First-Mate's Guide to Cruising the Inside Passage

Thriving and surviving the waters
from Olympia to Glacier Bay

by

Joanne Rodasta Wilshin

Anacortes, Washington

V🜨YAGER

Copyright © 2017 by Joanne Rodasta Wilshin.

All rights reserved. No part of this publication may be reproduced, distributed or transmitted in any form or by any means, without prior written permission by the author.

VOYAGER

A Voyager Book
519 Commercial Ste. 1942
Anacortes, WA 98221
joannewilshin.com

Publisher's Note: This book is not intended to be a substitute for professional maritime and nautical training and reference. Only government publications and regulations should be turned to for guidance for navigation and safety. The reader should always consult other sources for information found in this book. The author and publisher of this book intend for the information in this book to supplement, not replace, skillfully compiled maritime data and regulations.

Book Layout: P.B.Sargent/ Anacortes
Book Typography: Palantino by Hermann Zapf and Tahoma by Matthew Carter
Cover Design: P.B.Sargent/ Anacortes
Cover Typography: Optimus Princeps and Bastardus Sans by Manfred Klein, Allura by Robert E. Leuschke
Cover Photograph: Shutterstock
Author Photograph: Laurie Bryston/ Laguna Beach, California
Typography: Microsoft Palatino Linotype

The first-mate's guide to cruising the Inside Passage: thriving and surviving the waters from Olympia to Glacier Bay. Wilshin, Joanne Rodasta -- 1st ed.

ISBN 978-0692836194

To Davy

Acknowledgements

I thank our long-time Southern California cruising mates, Henry and Gail Salerno. We learned a lot in our fifteen years of sailing together.

I thank my husband, Dave Wilshin, an avid boatman and sailor. He showed much patience while I learned the ropes of off-shore and Inland Passage boating.

I thank the members of the Fidalgo Yacht Club in Anacortes, Washington. When we moved to Washington from Southern California, we had no idea how different our future boating experiences would be. For one thing, we went to the dark side by selling our beloved Mason 43 *Always* and buying a *L'Esprit*, our 44 Ocean Alexander. Going from sail to power in itself is a huge change. But going from Southern California waters to Pacific Northwest waters is also a huge change.

Our newfound yachties took us under their wings to help us adapt to both our new boat and our new environs. And for a group of seasoned and adventurous mariners, they knew a lot. I would especially like to thank Penny and Walt Barnard, Carl Bergan and Linda Page, Bob and Barbee Cromack, Carole Buffum and Ken Davis, Annette and Skip Hawk, Katherine and Rich Haynie, Sue and Don Hill, Janet Lien and Tom Hopper, Barb and Rob Hylton, Ellen Kaiser and the late Bob Lane, Stephanie and Fred Kaufhold, Barb and Wil Kerns, Dianne and Tom Kuhn, Kim and John McCollister, Martha and Ron McGough, Kim Adams and

Bill Monteforte, Fran and Dick Moore, Sherry and Eric Muller, Eugenia and Bob Murphy, Marlene and Jim Niehaus, Herb and Joanne Nyquist, Irene and Mark Perry, Mike Sharp, Jan and Jerry Schutzler, Joni and Charlie Simmerman, Judy and Jim Templeman, Diane and Bob Thompson, Joann and Dennis Thornton, Gary Walls and Bill Healy, Cindy and Dave Watt, Liz and Wayne Weideman, Joanne and David Witiak, and Elaine and David York.

Also helpful to us have been our Canadian friends from the Capitol City Yacht Club in Sidney on Vancouver Island. I send a special thank-you to Joan and Daryl Kyba.

And last, I thank my son Nicolas Rodasta, a licensed sea captain who taught me some very interesting lessons about cruising.

Table of Contents

1 Welcome, First Mates! - 11
PLANNING YOUR CRUISE
2 Types of Cruising - 26
3 Cruising Areas - 37
4 Sharing and Organizing the Responsibilities - 58
PREPARING TO CRUISE
5 The Boat Notebook - 72
6 Life-Preserving and Safety Equipment - 76
7 Sound and Light-Producing Devices - 85
8 The Boat Library - 90
9 Provisioning the Galley - 96
10 The Healthy and Safe Boat - 114
11 Cruise Communications - 127
12 Insurance - 156
13 Finances and Mail - 160
14 Your Boat's Fluids - 167
15 Tool Kits - 172
16 Managing Customs - 179
17 The Float Plan - 189

ENJOYING YOUR CRUISE

18 Understanding the Waters - 196

19 Navigating the Waters - 214

20 Understanding the Weather - 245

21 Anchoring - 254

22 Docking - 269

23 Fair Winds - 279

APPENDICES

Cruising Terminology - 281

Main Marine-Radio Channels - 286

Horn Blasts - 288

Marine-Radio Lingo - 289

Marine-Radio Scripts - 290

About the Author - 296

Index – 297

Chapter One

Welcome, First Mates!

The Three Phases of Cruising ★ Information You Can Trust
What's a First Mate?

This book is what I wished I had when, as first-mate aboard *L'Esprit*, I set out to cruise the Pacific Northwest in 2011 with my husband Dave.

At the time, I had very little idea of just how different cruising in the Inside Passage was from anything else I'd experienced in my previous twenty years of cruising the Southern California, Baja, and Chesapeake waters.

On the plus side, what I immediately discovered was that cruising in the PNW is like being an actor in a luscious National Geographic adventure series. Here's why I think that:

You and the Captain can cruise around literally hundreds of drop-dead-gorgeous pine and cedar-covered islands that dot the seas from Washington to British Columbia and Alaska.

A lot of these islands are inhabited full-time, so they have marinas where you can play, get fed, pick up supplies, use

Wi-Fi, and compare notes and adventures with other cruisers.

There're also plenty of uninhabited islands where you can anchor and let your inner Robinson Crusoe come out to play.

The abundance of fish, especially salmon and halibut, as well as crab and prawns, draw a fascinating variety of wildlife to the waters you'll be cruising. You'll be smitten by the many eagles, whales, orcas, bears, otters, seals, and birdlife that go about their daily lives so near your boat.

And, yes, all that fish is available for you to eat if you have the equipment and licenses necessary.

Last, you'll love the vivid sunsets, and the dynamic cloud-filled, Kodachrome blue skies. You'll love the photographs you take. You'll love how the air smells. And hopefully, you'll love your PNW cruising adventure(s).

But, to be frank, compared to cruising in other parts of the world, the PNW is quite like a video game. The waters are filled with things to avoid and obstacles that appear suddenly from the right or the left. You never know what you'll meet in the water or what might spring from behind an island: logs, kayakers, whales, gill netters, ferries, tugs towing barges or log booms, and huge ocean liners.

As a result, there are some things you and the Captain will want to fully understand in order to make safe, comfortable passages:

You'll want to understand and be prepared for conditions that arise when huge amounts of water ebb and flood around thousands of islands: rapids, narrows, whirlpools, standing waves, and copious amounts of logs (water forests!).

The weather will be an active player in your cruising experiences. You'll want to understand it so you can make it your friend.

Going from Washington to Canada and on to SE Alaska, and then back again, requires adjusting to each area's navigation charts and aids, as well as clocks, radio frequencies, and even the phone you use.

You'll have a much more rewarding adventure if you and the Captain arm yourselves with as much knowledge as possible before you set out. When you're cruising in the PNW, ignorance is not bliss.

Which is exactly what this book is for: Giving you the tools to thrive and survive cruising in the Inside Passage waters of the Pacific Northwest.

The Three Phases of Cruising

This book is organized especially to help you, the First Mate, know what you'll mostly likely need to plan for and to know on your cruise, whether it's a one- or two-week charter, or a longer cruise lasting a month or more, and whether you're on a sailboat or a power boat.

It's also organized so you can quickly look up information to jog your memory. There's a lot in here, so I'm guessing there's no way you're going to remember it all. I want to give you the peace of mind that comes from knowing where to get the information and helpful hints you'll need.

This book has three major sections: 1) Planning Your Cruise, 2) Preparing to Cruise, and 3) Enjoying Your Cruise.

At the beginning of each chapter, I'll frame the information you'll be reading about by telling you what motivates me to share the information I do. This usually has to do with safety and comfort, because when those needs are met, enjoying the cruise increases dramatically.

Planning Your Cruise

These three chapters include the things you'll want to think about and acquire before you seriously think about provisioning your boat and make cruising preparations. These things are:

- Types of Cruising
- Cruising Areas
- Sharing and Organizing the Responsibilities (including a helpful list of cruising tasks)

Preparing to Cruise

These twelve chapters include all the things you'll need to consider when preparing your boat and yourselves for your actual cruise, regardless of whether you're going on a long or short cruise. These chapters deal with preparing yourselves and your boat for the experiences you will encounter and for having a safe and healthy journey. For maximum comfort and safety, attend to these topics BEFORE you leave:

- The Boat Notebook
- Life-preserving and Safety Equipment
- Sound and Light Making Equipment
- The Boat Library
- Provisioning the Galley
- A Healthful, Safe Boat
- Cruising Communications (including marine-radio scripts)

- Insurance
- Finances and Mail
- Your Boat's Fluids
- Tool Kits
- Preparing for Customs
- Float Plan

Enjoying Your Cruise

The last five chapters provide you information, suggestions, and resources to help you drive your boat and to optimize your living conditions while underway. Read them before you leave; utilize them while you're underway.

- Understanding the Waters
- Navigating the Waters (including rules of the road)
- Making Friends with the Weather
- Anchoring (including rafting)
- Docking

At the end of many chapters are suggestions for pages you'll want to include in your Boat Notebook, which I'll explain pretty soon. Templates for many of these pages can be accessed from my website FirstMatesGuide.com.

Information You Can Trust

The advice in this book is gleaned from my own experience and from discussions with many veteran cruisers we've met on our travels, as well as my fellow seafaring members of Fidalgo Yacht Club, in Anacortes, Washington.

The members of this club are primarily cruisers who venture near and far each spring and summer. I used to joke when I first joined the club that when the weather started warming up, they all headed north. They're a smart and hardy bunch!

Many of these Fidalgo Yacht Club members consider a 250-nautical-mile round trip pretty normal. Collectively, they have an incomparable breadth of knowledge and experience regarding the PNW waters. My husband Dave and I owe them much gratitude for what they have taught us and for the dangers from which they've kept us safe.

In 2016 we were one of five club boats who travelled separately to Alaska, and met up here and there along the way. In 2015 ten club boats made the roundtrip to SE Alaska. An equal number ventured beyond Cape Caution to British Columbia's pristine Central Coast and visited Shearwater and Ocean Falls. As I said, it is a cruising club extraordinaire! I benefitted from their knowledge, and so will you.

What's a First Mate?

While the Captain of your vessel is the one who ultimately assumes responsibility for running the boat, being your vessel's First Mate means you're the ultra-important second-person-in-charge.

And I mean that!

You are second-in-charge, and therefore vitally important. Here's why.

On a cruising boat, the title Captain, like First Mate, does not come with pre-defined jobs. The Captain could be the one who tends to the engine and decides the routes. But not necessarily. I know plenty of cruising couples whose First Mate is the chief navigator or the engine mechanic, while the Captain is the one who does laundry in port or prepares meals.

So be flexible when divvying up the responsibilities.

When dividing up the tasks, figure out which responsibilities work best for you and which work best for the Captain. Factor in each other's strengths and weaknesses when doing this, and be open to changing some roles when needed.

For instance, many crews might think it logical that the First Mate do all the line handling. On our boat, we don't. I'm afraid of the water because of a childhood incident, so my husband Capt. Dave is the one who goes on the forward deck to raise the anchor and coil up the docking lines when we leave port. Despite my fear, I have trained myself to step onto the dock to tie up our boat to the cleats or bull rails.

In chapter four I give a pretty thorough, but general, list of the jobs needing to be divided up. You'll probably discover some that I haven't listed, and you'll probably find there are some that don't apply to your boat. Be sure to refer to that list.

As First Mate and second-in-charge, you'll want to be prepared for three levels of functioning:

- Doing your First-Mate tasks.
- Relieving the Captain in emergencies.
- Being a valued Second Opinion.

In order to fulfill these functions, you'll want to build toward having a good sense of:

- When things are going right.
- When things are going wrong, or potentially going wrong.

- Where to look for help.
- What to do to be helpful.
- What the Captain's jobs are and how to do them in case you have to take over in some form.
- How to give your jobs to someone else to do.

Be prepared for your first-mate's tasks

There's a lot to do on a boat before, during and after a passage. Spreading the load of all those tasks between you and the Captain goes a long way to ease the stress of boating.

On *L'Esprit*, for example, it's Capt. Dave's job to: 1) go though his engine-room inspection check list before we ever turn on our twin Detroits, 2) bring up the anchor or untie the mooring lines, and then 3) coil the lines and bring up the fenders while I prepare to drive the boat away.

My First-Mate jobs while Capt. Dave's busy with his tasks are to make sure everything we need for our passage (charts, electronics, radios, coffee, binoculars, camera, notepad, etc.) are at the helm station and easily accessible during our passage. I also start the engines and make sure all the switches and dials (navigation lights, GPS, auto-pilot, etc.) are in their proper on or off positions.

You might wonder how I do this without messing up. Here's the answer.

I have a Boat Notebook on board, a loose-leaf binder that contains all this information in case I experience a memory lapse. After a winter of non-boating, it amazes me the simple things I forget.

The notebook also includes instructions and drawings that detail Capt. Dave's tasks. I took the time to follow Capt.

Dave around and have him describe step-by-step how he does certain boat operations.

I've never regretted the time I took to list how to turn on and off the engines and the generator, or the effort I took to make drawings that show how the electrical panel should look when we're at a dock, at anchorage, and underway. I rarely look at this information, but when I need it, I know where to easily find it.

For example, it's Capt. Dave's job to operate our water maker. Knowing that an emergency could arise while the water-maker's running, I have a page in my notebook detailing how to turn the system on and off. Those instructions and their accompanying diagrams have definitely come in handy a couple of times.

The Boat Notebook is also there for the times we have guests on board who suddenly, because of an emergency, have needed the notebook's information. I know it's ready for them and trust that they'll be able to use the information.

As for the learning curve required to become an adept First-Mate, I say: Be kind to yourself while constantly improving your skills through practice and discussions. The Captain won't do everything perfectly either, if that's a consolation. But you both want the best outcomes. So whenever you think your skills failed you, sit down with the Captain and talk about ways to become and feel more successful.

Capt. Dave and I often do this after docking maneuvers so we can help each other do our best as a team when docking and undocking *L'Esprit*. For example, because I often have a difficult time grabbing the mid-ship line when docking, Capt. Dave made a special line for me. He rigged a landing line that started at the mid-ship cleat and traveled to the aft where it was held by a cam cleat. That way, when I get off L'*Esprit*'s swim step with the stern line, I can easily grab the tail end of the mid-ship line that is now at the stern.

This is just one of a myriad number of examples of how discussing a problem resulted in a working solution and an improvement in my skills.

Relieve the captain in emergencies

Now for the kicker: The reason I previously described the First Mate as an ultra-important position is that as First Mate, you'll have times when you need to step in for the Captain in an emergency.

Maybe it's as simple as the Captain needing a bathroom break.

Or it's more complicated: the Captain becomes suddenly nauseated, or he gets hurt, or he falls overboard.

That's why even though you may not be the primary navigator or boat driver, you'll need to at least learn how to do those things in case an emergency arises, just as he'll need to know how to do your jobs in case something happens to you.

You'll need to know, for example, how to steer the boat, use the radio to hail help, shut the boat down and start it up. This book will help you with that. Among other things, it will give you:

- Driving exercises to do to make you feel more competent. (Ch. 19)
- Marine-radio scripts to help you speak with the Coast Guard and other boats, including large ships, as well as with marinas. (Ch. 11)

- A system for organizing a Boat Notebook to easily access needed information. (Ch. 6)

When Capt. Dave and I first started cruising in the PNW, the thought of taking over in an emergency overwhelmed me. Doing so seemed so much easier when we were sailing off the coast of California. But then, the coast of California is not a video game. It's straight forward. It's big and open. There are no logs or narrow passages or suddenly-shallow areas through which to navigate.

Yet I knew that if we were to successfully cruise the PNW waters, I had some learning ahead of me. I had to have some working knowledge of *L'Esprit*'s electrical system, and I had to know how to turn on and off the engines and generator and water maker. The rules of the road and speaking radio-talk had to become second nature to me. (Even if you're chartering for a week or two, you'll still want to quickly find the basic rules of the road and the marine-radio scripts in this book.)

Why would I want to know all this?

If something happens to Capt. Dave, our survival depends on me taking over the boat and getting her and us to safety and aid.

I have to admit it took me a while, but I did it. And it wasn't always pretty either.

So, you don't need to know how to do everything perfectly. You just need to know enough to stabilize a difficult situation. You'll improve through practice, and you'll get that practice by taking over tasks. Be the one who calls marinas for slips. Be the one who navigates or drives through narrows. For a First-Mate, knowledge is power, and ignorance is not bliss.

That's why this book has sections that provide: easily adaptable marine-radio scripts, first-aid and ship-traffic information, and suggested publications to have on board for emergency situations.

By the way, I wish you many wonderful sails and no emergency situations.

Be the second opinion

We all make mistakes, even the Captain. Sometimes this is funny, like when he steers the boat in the wrong direction, or he forgets to cleat off a sheet. But sometimes it's not funny at all. He doesn't put out enough scope on the anchor and your boat drags, or he forgets to adjust the time when calculating currents and you find yourself facing water coming against you at seven-knots. Trust me, these things happen.

Because mistakes can cause real problems while cruising, you'll want to learn as much as you can to offer the Captain your valued second opinion. Or at least have the resources to provide helpful second opinions. In this book, you'll learn about weather parameters, current calculation short cuts, and the rules of the road, all of which help you in times when questionable situations arise.

You don't have to memorize this information. Just bring this book with you when cruising, and look up information when you need it.

PLANNING YOUR CRUISE

Chapter Two

Planning Your Cruise

Types of Cruising

Sail vs. Power ★ Chartering vs. Owning
Local vs. Long Distance ★ Urban vs. Wilderness

The first time you find yourself at a PNW marina chatting with other boaters, you'll discover their stories differ considerably. You're just as likely to meet cruisers who've sailed up from Australia or Mexico as you are to meet locals who've never motored more than thirty miles in any direction. You'll meet sailors, and you'll meet power boaters. You'll meet boaters who're only in the marina because they need to restock their galleys from the grocery store, or you'll meet cruisers who haven't used their anchor in a couple of years. You'll meet people from Texas and Tennessee who've chartered a boat for a week or two, and you'll meet boaters on their way home from a couple of months in SE Alaska or beyond.

Each of these cruising styles requires different skills and planning. Regardless, both power boaters and sailors should know the basics of:

- Weather and sea forecasting
- Rules of the road
- Radio speak
- Navigation
- Man-overboard maneuvers
- Anchoring
- Docking
- Customs requirements

Sail or Power

Sailboats

When Capt. Dave and I first moved to the PNW, we were advised that most cruisers owned power boats. Experience has taught me that's a myth: plenty of sailors cruise the whole Inside Passage, and they manage just fine. In fact, they enjoy the heck out of their experiences. So it matters not whether you cruise on a sailboat or power boat; with a few exceptions, the information in this book will apply to both sailors and power boaters.

If you're cruising on a sailboat, it might take you longer to reach each destination, but you'll use less fuel, and, if you're lucky, you'll get in a good sail on the way. As First Mate, you'll want to pay special attention to:

- Basic sailing maneuvers.
- Rules of the road for sailboats.
- Provisioning and storage.
- Food preparation.

- Water acquisition and storage.

If your sailboat has an inboard engine or has auxiliary power driven by wind or solar, you may have an electrical system that supports lights, electronics, and refrigeration, all of which make distance cruising easier. As First Mate, you'll also want to know about:

- Your boat's electrical panel.
- Troubleshooting engine, electrical, and plumbing problems.
- Fueling station locations.

Dave and I have chatted with plenty of adventurous and enthusiastic small-boat cruisers whose only means of propulsion besides their sails is an outboard motor. If this is you, as First Mate you'll want to know about

- Foods that store well.
- Camp cooking.
- Alternate power supplies.

Power Boats

Besides the basics, if your cruising chariot is a power boat, you'll want to know about:

- Provisioning and storage.
- Food preparation.
- Troubleshooting engine, electrical, and plumbing problems.
- Fueling station locations.
- Water acquisition and storage.
- Driving a single-engine boat versus driving a twin-engine boat.

Chartering or Owning

Chartering

Chartering is a great way to learn about what you like in a boat while also experiencing the PNW waters, perhaps for the first time. An advantage of chartering is obvious: You only have to pay to use the boat for a specific amount of time. But with that comes responsibilities. The charterer will expect you to return the boat the way you got it in the first place. No dings. No accidents.

If you choose to charter, do business with a reputable company. There are plenty of them in Washington, Canada, and Alaska. *Waggoner Cruising Guide* mentions many of them.

Most chartering companies will expect you to know the basics of boat handling, navigating, and rules of the road. Don't be surprised if they ask you for your boating resume. Also, there are on-line courses you can take to beef up your resume, as well as your personal knowledge and confidence.

If you have no experience whatsoever, consider hiring a captain and possibly a crew to accompany you on your cruise, or at least the first part of your cruise.

Before you leave the dock, the chartering company will give you a very complete run-through of the boat before you depart, during which I'd advise you, the First Mate, to write everything (!!) down in a notebook of some sort. Don't assume you'll remember everything; you probably won't.

If you read this book before you go, you'll have enough knowledge to ask pertinent questions before you leave the dock. It's better to have your answers at the dock than out at sea.

Also remember that when you charter, they may advise you where you cannot go, which is mostly for insurance reasons. Like most cruising grounds, there are places where you can get into trouble if you lack enough local knowledge.

Last, have a great time! Capt. Dave and I moved to the PNW because we chartered a boat out of Anacortes and cruised in the San Juan and Gulf Islands. It was one of my favorite vacations ever.

Ownership

With owning or co-owning your own boat, comes freedom to travel when and where you wish.

It also gives you all the responsibilities of ownership: maintenance, upgrading, and liability.

As First Mate, you'll want to be as knowledgeable as possible about every aspect of your boat because:

- You may have to describe a boat problem to a mechanic or the Coast Guard.
- You'll want to help your Captain make the best decisions regarding the boat.
- You'll want to have enough knowledge so when something unusual happens, say you sense a new smell, or there's a weird knocking sound, you'll know to discuss it with the Captain.

Naturally, becoming knowledgeable about your boat will take time. So be kind to yourself. At the same time, listen to conversations the Captain has with other boat owners and with your boat's mechanic. Ask questions.

Make sure there's a copy of Nigel Calder's *Boatowner's Mechanical and Electrical Manual: How to Maintain,*

Repair, and Improve Your Boat's Essential Systems on board. (We have a copy at home too.)

If you open up the book, you'll notice that the chapters include troubleshooting flow-charts. As First-Mate, you'll be a great help to the Captain if you read him the troubleshooting steps while he's in the process of figuring out what problem needs solving. Or the Captain can read to you if you're the on-board engine specialist.

Nigel Calder's book also helps you become aware of your boat's systems and how they interrelate. When you have some idle time, leaf through it. It really will start making sense, even though the vocabulary might not be what you're used to at first.

As First Mate, you'll also want to be in on where you travel. A great book to help you with this, and something you'll want to keep on your boat, is the most current *Waggoner Cruising Guide*. This guide is updated and published annually. You do not want to leave port without it.

You'll also want to have last year's copy at home. We keep our home copy in a kitchen drawer so we can easily refer to it when we're chatting about destinations over dinner. Also, consider asking your local printer to re-bind your copy of *Waggoner* with spiral binding. It'll be easier to handle when you're underway.

The *Waggoner Guide* covers every marina and anchorage from Olympia to Ketchikan, and the west side of Vancouver Island. You'll read what to expect when you get to each spot and whether other cruisers love the spot or not. Plus there are pages and pages of information regarding marine radio channels, rules of the road, weather stations, getting through rapids and around Cape Caution or past Dixon Entrance. It's truly the most up-to-date and thorough cruising guide you'll find for cruising on the Pacific Northwest waters.

If SE Alaska is part of your cruising itinerary, you'll want to include the most recent edition of *Northwest Boat Travel*. Like the *Waggoner Guide*, it includes tons of information about all the anchorages and marinas along the Inside passage. Unlike *Waggoner*, it covers SE Alaska beyond Ketchikan, which *Waggoner* does not.

A good online resource for much of this information is ActiveCaptain.com. Consider joining (free!) so you can enjoy all the first-hand knowledge other members provide on this well-organized boating site.

Besides Nigel Calder's and the *Waggoner* books, there are other books, computer programs, and Internet resources to help you cruise and operate your boat. In chapter eight, you'll find a long list of these, and throughout this book you'll read about what many of these provide. You don't need all the books, but you'll definitely need an assortment for your boat's library. Remember, knowledge is power!

Local or Long-Distance Cruising

Local cruising

Local Cruising is a lot easier than long-distance cruising:

You probably won't have to go through customs, which would take some planning before you proceed on a boat.

Provisioning is easier because you'll probably be gone for a shorter time.

You're near enough to home that if there is an emergency, you can more easily take care of it, which is not always the case when long-distance cruising.

You're probably traveling no farther than fifty miles in any one direction, so you still have the feeling of being in your own backyard.

Some of the favorite local places Washingtonians like to cruise are:

- The San Juan Islands.
- The islands off Seattle.
- The islands surrounding Olympia.
- Favorite places for Vancouverites are:
- The Gulf Islands.
- The Sunshine Coast.
- The islands of Georgia Strait.
- Campbell River Canadians venture to:
- Desolation Sound.
- The Discovery Islands.
- The Broughtons.

As you'll read in this book, all the above areas are unique and have to be prepared for a bit differently. Some areas have more marinas, some have fewer. Some areas you can count on for easy access to groceries, water, and fuel, others you can't.

Thus, an advantage of local cruising is that you only have to think about what you need for a specific area, rather than preparing for several different ones.

Also, you probably won't have to make passages across difficult waterways. But if you do, be sure to factor in waiting time for crossings that include the Strait of Georgia, Cape Caution, and Dixon Entrance. The wait time allows you to make these crossings in fair weather, rather than poor and uncomfortable conditions. In others words, travel these waters when the weather and wave heights will be relatively calm. If the forecast is not in your favor, wait, even if it's for days. You'll thank me for telling you this!

Long-distance cruising

Long-distance cruises are ones in which you:

- Visit more than one of the above areas.
- Are gone anywhere from three weeks to four or five months.

Long-distance cruises take planning, knowledge, and time. As First Mate, you'll not want to leave on one of these cruises without having first planned out your:

- Budget.
- Timeline.
- Boat needs.
- Personal needs.

You'll want to be acquainted with the:

- Waters.
- Weather patterns.
- Places to fuel up.
- Places to provision.
- Medical assistance available in the area.
- All spots that provide refuge.

You'll want to have a handle on:

- Communications, because they vary as you move out of one area and into another.

- Insurance needs and limitations, because you'll need to make sure your policy lets you go where you want.

This book will guide you, the First Mate, through this so you feel organized and on top of things. You don't have to have everything memorized, but you will want to know where to locate the information you need when you need it.

Urban or Wilderness Cruising

One last type of cruising differentiates between cruising in urban areas, as opposed to wilderness areas. I define urban cruising as going from marina to marina. Sometimes these so-called urban areas are out in the middle of the wilderness. For example, when in the Broughtons, you can go from marina to marina without ever spending a night at anchor in a wilderness bay.

When urban cruising, you'll be going to marinas where you can find water, electricity, and perhaps fuel and Wi-Fi. There'll probably be a store from which you can provision, and even a pub. When you look in your *Waggoner Cruising Guide* or *Northwest Boat Travel*, you'll be able to read about all their amenities.

Wilderness cruising, on the other hand, means you're pretty much on your own. You'll need to set your anchor correctly, or you'll float away. You'll need to provide your own energy for cooking and lights. If you run out of water and don't have a water maker, well then, you're pretty much out of water. (Actually there are a couple of spots, like Roscoe Bay and Melanie Cove in Desolation Sound, in which cruisers have installed a pipe to siphon mountain run-off water.)

Usually on your cruises you'll try for a combination of both urban and wilderness experiences. Personally, after five or six days of being at anchor, I want to get to a marina. But after maybe two or three days tied to a marina, I really want to get back to a rustic anchorage. You'll soon learn what your and the Captain's thresholds are and will plan your trips accordingly.

Resources
For Navigation and Amenities

- Waggoner Cruising Guide
- Northwest Boat Travel
- ActiveCaptain.com

For Boat Maintenance

- Nigel Calder's *Boatowner's Mechanical and Electrical Manual,* fourth edition
- World Cruising Wiki's Yacht Maintenance List (cruiserswiki.org > Wiki Contents >Yacht Maintenance).

Chapter 3

Planning Your Cruise

Cruising Areas

South Puget Sound ★ North Puget Sound
The San Juan Islands Area ★ The Gulf Islands area
The Sunshine Coast Area ★ North Georgia Strait
Desolation Sound & Discovery Islands area
The Broughtons and Vicinity
British Columbia's North Coast ★ SE Alaska

Once you know what type of cruising you'll be planning for, you'll need to decide where you'll be cruising.

Depending on where you live, the following areas, from south to north, are all considered part of the Pacific Northwest's Inside Passage.

I urge you to get yourself at least two copies of *Waggoner Cruising Guide*—one for the boat and one for home. If you plan to go to SE Alaska, definitely add the *Northwest Boat Travel* guide.

Here I give you a brief sampling of the ten major cruising areas of the Inside Passage (so called because you can travel more than eight-hundred miles to Southeast Alaska with only a few passages in the open Pacific waters).

South Puget Sound

South Puget Sound spans from Olympia, Washington, up through the Seattle area and west of Whidbey Island to Port Townsend and its adjacent coves. It's warmer here in the summer, and is more urban, which doesn't mean it has no quiet, rustic getaways. It has plenty. You'll have a wide variety of experiences from visiting Washington's state capital, to docking next to the Chihuly museum and Hot Shop (my favorite!), to taking in Bainbridge Island's weekend farmer's market. Port Townsend is known for its wooden boats, and if you go to Bell Harbor in downtown Seattle, you can experience the city sites and even take in a ball game with the stadiums nearby.

What to enjoy

- Tacoma museums by the waterfront: Chihuly Glass Museum, Tacoma Museum of Art, Tacoma Historical Museum, and Car Museum (requires a walk).
- Bell Town's sports arenas, shopping, Ferris wheel, and the Space Needle.
- Port Townsend's Wooden Boat Chandlery and Northwest Marine Center.
- Olympia's state capitol building.
- Poulsbo's Little Norway.
- Bremerton's USS Turner Joy and Puget Sound Navy Museum.
- Hood Canal.

- Kayaking; hiking; seasonal fishing, crabbing, and prawning; birding.
- The Hiram M. Chittenden Locks, or Ballard Locks, taking you to Lakes Union and Washington.

What to watch out for

- Maritime Military activity near Keyport.
- Rapids (Agate Passage, The Narrows).
- Ship and ferry traffic.
- Fog.
- Fishing boats.
- Navigational aids.

Helpful publications

- Current Waggoner Cruising Guide (Fine Edge).
- Current *Northwest Boat Travel* (Vernon Pub).
- *Puget Sound - A Boater's Guide: First* Edition (Yeardon-Jones).
- Current year's Puget Sound Tides and Current book.
- Fine Edge's *Ports and Passes*.
- *The Burgee* – guide to marinas.
- Charts.

Internet resources

- Google: Cruising South Puget Sound.
- BellHarbor.com.
- DockStreetMarina.com.
- ActiveCaptain.com.
- CruisingNW.com.
- WaggonerGuide.com, Updates.
- BoatTravel.com, Chapters 1-4.

- NWCruising.net.
- PassageMaker.com, Pacific Northwest.
- CruisingWorld.com.
- NWYachting.com.
- NWBoatInfo.com.

North Puget Sound

North Puget extends from the south end of Whidbey Island to Oak Harbor and La Conner.

What to enjoy

- Langley's antique shops.
- Oak Harbor's naval facilities.
- Coupeville
- La Conner's shopping and Museum of Northwest Art.
- Kayaking; hiking; seasonal fishing, crabbing, and prawning; birding.

What to watch out for

- Watch buoy markers when entering and passing through the sometimes-shallow Oak Harbor entrance.
- The strong, eddying currents under Desolation Pass Bridge need to be timed before passing.
- Strong currents in La Conner.
- Crab and prawn traps.
- Small fishing boats.
- Ferry and tug-and-barge traffic.

Helpful publications

- Current *Waggoner Cruising Guide* (Fine Edge).

- Current *Northwest Boat Travel* (Vernon Pub.).
- *Puget Sound - A Boater's Guide*: First Edition (Yeardon-Jones).
- Current year's Puget Sound Tides and Current book.
- Fine Edge's *Ports and Passes*.
- *The Burgee* – guide to marinas.
- Charts.

Internet resources

- ActiveCaptain.com.
- VisitLangley.com.
- LoveLaConner.com.
- CruisingNW.com.
- WaggonerGuide.com, Updates.
- BoatTravel.com, Chapter 5.
- NWCruising.net.
- PassageMaker.com, Pacific Northwest.
- CruisingWorld.com.
- NWYachting.com.
- NWBoatInfo.com.

San Juan Islands, Including Anacortes and Bellingham

The San Juan Islands lie east of Victoria, north of Whidbey Island, and southwest of the city of Vancouver on Canada's mainland. These gorgeous islands are a major tourist attraction of northwest Washington. Not only are there plenty of anchorages and marinas, you'll also see eagles and orcas. If you're from Canada, you'll need to go through customs.

What to enjoy

- On Orcas Island, Rosario Resort.
- On Lopez Island, Fisherman's Resort.
- On San Juan Island, Roche and Friday Harbors.
- Bellingham's historic Fairhaven district, via shuttle.
- Semiahmoo Resort north of Bellingham.
- Anacortes's Old Town and maritime building industry.
- Kayaking; hiking; seasonal fishing, crabbing, and prawning; birding.

What to watch out for

- Ferries making abrupt turns around landings.
- Ship and tug traffic in Rosario Strait.
- Strong currents at Deception Pass.
- Crap and prawn traps.
- Logs and deadheads.
- Kayakers.
- Wind against current in Rosario Strait.
- Eddies off Speiden and southwest Lopez Islands.
- Watch buoy markers when entering and passing through the sometimes-shallow Swinomish Channel.

Helpful publications

- *Dreamspeaker Vol. 4 - The San Juan Islands* (buy through Fine Edge Publishing).
- *Waggoner Cruising Guide.*
- *Northwest Boat Travel.*
- San Juan Islands map from Fine Edge (shows where to anchor!)

- *The Burgee* – guide to marinas.
- Fine Edge's *Ports and Passes*.
- The Washington State Ferry Schedule, published quarterly.
- Charts.

Internet resources

- VisitSanJuans.com.
- Wikipedia topic: San Juan Islands.
- Washington Ferry schedule (wsdot.wa.gov/ferries).
- Anacortes.org.
- Bellingham.org.
- WaggonerGuide.com, Updates.
- BoatTravel.com, Chapters 6-7.
- NWCruising.net.
- PassageMaker.com, Pacific Northwest.
- CruisingWorld.com.
- NWYachting.com.
- NWBoatInfo.com.

Gulf Islands

These Canadian Islands and surrounds include the southeastern quarter of Vancouver Island, including Victoria, Sidney, Chemainus, and Nanaimo, as well as nearly two hundred islands, big and small, including Saltspring, Galiano, and Gabriola Islands.

What to enjoy

- Ganges on Saltspring Island, including its Saturday farmers' market.
- Cowachin Bay Marine Center.

- Genoa Bay.
- Butchart Gardens.
- Victoria – Royal British Columbia Museum and the Empress Hotel.
- The murals of Chemainus and the Chemainus Theatre.
- Hummingbird Pub on Galiano Island.
- Kayaking; hiking; seasonal fishing, crabbing, and prawning; birding.

What to watch out for

- Logs and tugs with log booms.
- Kayaks.
- Sea planes.
- Ship traffic and their wakes in Haro Strait and Boundary Pass.
- Strong currents that need to be timed in Samsum and Dodd Narrows and Gabriola and Porlier Passes.

Helpful publications

- *Dreamspeaker Vol. 1 — Gulf Islands and Vancouver Island* (buy through Fine Edge Publishing).
- *Waggoner Cruising Guide.*
- *Northwest Boat Travel.*
- *The Burgee* – guide to marinas.
- Gulf Islands map from Fine Edge (shows where to anchor!)
- Fine Edge's *Ports and Passes.*
- Canadian Tides and Current Tables, Volume 5.

- The ferry schedule for the Gulf Islands and vicinity.

Internet resources

- ActiveCaptain.
- GulfIslandsGuide.com.
- Wikipedia topic: Gulf Islands.
- SidneyBC.org.
- TourismVictoria.com.
- VisitChemainus.ca.
- TourismLadysmith.ca.
- MapleBayMarina.com.
- ExploreNanimoBC.com.
- WaggonerCruisingGuide.com, Updates.
- BoatTravel.com, Chapters 9-11.
- NWCruising.net.
- PassageMaker.com, Pacific Northwest.
- CruisingWorld.com.
- NWYachting.com.
- NWBoatInfo.com.

Sunshine Coast, Including Vancouver

The Sunshine Coast extends from the city of Vancouver on the British Columbia mainland northward, and includes Pender Harbour, Princess Louise, Powell River, and Lund, which is at the terminus of the Pan American Highway.

What to enjoy

- Vancouver Museum of Anthropology.
- Princess Louise Inlet and Chatterbox Falls
- Pender Harbour.
- Secret Harbour.

- Westview.
- The Copeland Islands.
- Lund Bakery.

What to watch out for

- Wind-against-current situations in the Strait of Georgia.
- Strong outflows into the Strait of Georgia from the Frazier River and Jervis Inlet.
- Logs and dead heads in the water.
- Ship and tug traffic.

Helpful publications

- *Dreamspeaker Vol. 3 - Vancouver, Howe Sound and the Sunshine Coast.*
- *Waggoner Cruising Guide.*
- *Northwest Boat Travel.*
- Inside Passage - South Portion folded map (Fine Edge).
- *Exploring Puget Sound and British Columbia,* Stephen E. Hilson, Ed.
- Fine Edge's *Ports and Passes.*

Internet resources

- ActiveCaptain.com.
- TourismVancouver.com.
- SunshineCoastCanada.com.
- SecheltVisitorCentre.com
- PenderHarbour.ca.
- LundBC.ca.
- PowellRiverDirect.com.
- WaggonerGuide.com, Updates

- BoatTravel.com, Chapters 12-13
- NWCruising.net.
- PassageMaker.com, Pacific Northwest
- CruisingWorld.com.
- NWYachting.com.
- NWBoatInfo.com.

Northern Georgia Strait

Several large islands stud Georgia Strait's northern section. These islands include Denman and Hornby Islands to the west, and Lesqueti and Texada Islands to the east. Comox is the largest town on the east side of Vancouver Island, north of Nanaimo and south of Campbell River.

The islands are far less urban than the islands to the south, and the passages from island to island are longer. Listen to weather reports, including buoy reports before departing. If the weather is not in your favor, stay put, especially when south-easterlies are predicted. These waters can become adverse quickly.

What to enjoy

- The town of Comox.
- Tribune Bay.
- Sturt Bay on Texada's northeastern shore provides shelter when Malaspina Strait is untidy.

What to watch out for

- Comox bar's shallow waters, especially in a south easterly.
- Military area Whiskey Golf, just east of Nanaimo.

- Wind against current, especially near Cape Mudge and Qualicum. Avoid being out in a south easterly. Listen for Sentry Shoals weather buoy.
- Ship and tug-and-barge traffic.
- Logs and deadheads.

Helpful publications

- *Waggoner Cruising Guide.*
- *Northwest Boat Travel.*
- Charts.
- Fine Edge's *Ports and Passes.*

Internet resources

- ActiveCaptain.com.
- DiscoverComoxValley.com
- Texada.org.
- DenmanIsland.com.
- Lesqueti.ca.
- HornbyIsland.com.
- WaggonerGuide.com, Updates.
- BoatTravel.com, Ch. 13 and 15.
- NWCruising.net.
- PassageMaker.com, Pacific Northwest.
- CruisingWorld.com.
- NWYachting.com.
- NWBoatInfo.com

Desolation Sound and the Discovery Islands, Including Discovery Passage

This area, north of the Strait of Georgia and south of the Sonora Island, is a gorgeous and popular warm-water cruising playground. July and August are the most popular months as the weather is drier and warmer, and families bring their kids here for vacation time. These months also see lots of cruisers returning from Alaska and the Central Coast before the weather starts turning in September. There are fewer full-service marinas in this area than you might expect: Refuge Cove, Gorge Harbour, Heriot Bay, and the bustling Campbell River area.

What to enjoy

- Prideaux Haven.
- Grace Harbour.
- Gorge Harbour.
- Heriot Bay.
- Von Donop Marine Park.
- Toba Wilderness.
- Squirrel Cove.
- Refuge Cove.
- Roscoe Bay (time your entry).
- Campbell River.
- Octopus Islands.
- Campbell River.
- Heriot Bay.
- Pendrell Arm.

What to watch out for

- Very strong currents in Seymour and Surge Narrows. Hole in the Wall, Okisollo Channel, Johnstone Strait, White Passage, and Seymore Narrows. Time before making your passage.
- Rocks in narrow channels.
- Bears, wolves, and wildcats on land.
- Logs and deadheads.

- Kayaks and canoes.
- Fishing prohibitions.

Helpful publications

- *Waggoner Cruising Guide.*
- *Northwest Boat Travel.*
- Inside Passage map, South Portion (Fine Edge).
- Desolation Sound folded map from Fine Edge (shows where to anchor!).
- *Dreamspeaker Vol. 2 — Desolation Sound and the Discovery Islands.*
- Fine Edge's *Ports and Passes.*

Articles and blogs

- ActiveCaptain.com.
- DiscoveryIslands.ca.
- CampbellRiverTourism.com.
- WaggonerGuide.com, Updates.
- BoatTravel.com, Chapters 14 and 16.
- NWCruising.net.
- PassageMaker.com, Pacific Northwest.
- CruisingWorld.com.
- NWYachting.com.
- NWBoatInfo.com.

The Broughtons, Including Queen Charlotte Strait, Johnstone Strait, and NE Vancouver Island

The Broughton Archipelago is another popular cruising destination. Getting there can require more time because you really do have to include wait time so you can make your longer passages when the weather is in your favor and to pass through narrows and rapids during slack currents.

Cruising to the Broughtons requires that you time your passage either through Seymour Narrows by Campbell River, or you travel through a series of five rapids that must also be timed. We have friends that swear by the Seymour Narrows passage, but Capt. Dave and I really prefer the longer route through Dent and the other rapids because we think it's so much prettier.

When you get to the Broughtons, a large, versatile cruising ground opens up to you. There are marinas that put a lot of thought and energy into making your stay with them fun and comfortable. Some provide fuel and food supplies. Sullivan Bay is the only marina in the Broughtons that sells bottled alcohol. There are also plenty of coves and bays in which to anchor. The fishing, crabbing, and prawning are pretty spectacular. Stores in the Broughtons are usually still stocking up in mid-June. Keep that in mind when provisioning. And Port McNeill is just across Queen Charlotte Strait if you need medical or mechanical help, or a supermarket fix.

A note about the Broughton marinas: They love to have happy hours, so come prepared with hors d'oeuvres to share (more on this in the provisioning section of this book).

What to enjoy

- The marinas at Port Harvey, Lagoon Cove, Kwatsi, Echo Bay, Shawl Bay, Sullivan Bay, and Jennis Bay.
- Alert Bay's U'Mista Museum.
- The Finnish settlement of Sointula.
- Lacy Falls.

- Shoal Bay in Cordero Channel.
- Nimmo Bay Wilderness Resort.
- Dent Lodge.
- Billy Proctor's Museum.
- Port McNeill on Vancouver Island.
- Shoal Bay Pub.

What to watch out for

- Check charts for ebb and flow directions; they're not always going in the direction you'd assume.
- Strong currents that need timing in: Yuculta, Dent, Greenpointe, Whirlpool Rapids; Drury Inlet; Gillard Passage; Race and Current Passages; Grappler Sound; and Kenneth Passage.
- Logs and log booms.
- Kayaks and canoes.
- Tug with barges and ocean liners.
- Time entrance to Booker Lagoon. See *Waggoner*. The entrance is a fall, as well as a narrow. This means that if you go in or out at the wrong time you could meet a sudden drop in water level, or you could meet a hill of water, which is an issue with lagoons. There is an anchorage just outside Booker Lagoon where you can wait for a beneficial time for your passage in or out.
- Read *Waggoner* before driving through Beware Passage.
- Time and watch range markers in Chatham Channel
- Tide lines during spring tides.

Helpful publications

- *Waggoner Cruising Guide.*
- *Northwest Boat Travel.*
- *Dreamspeaker Vol. 5 - The Broughtons.*
- *Local Knowledge* (K. Moynihan).
- *Proven Cruising Routes, Vol. 1 - Seattle to Ketchikan.*
- *Ports and Passes* or *Canadian Tides and Current Tables, V. 6 and 7.*
- *Exploring the South Coast of British Columbia* (Douglass).
- Inside Passage (chart) - South Portion.

Articles and blogs

- ActiveCaptain.com.
- Ahoybc.com, then click Explore or Blogbook.
- WaggonerGuide.com, Updates.
- DesolationSoundYachtCharters.com > Cruising Area > Itineraries.
- SeriousCharterer.wordpress.com.
- WaggonerCruisingGuide.com, Updates.
- BoatTravel.com, Chapter 17.
- NWCruising.net.
- PassageMaker.com, Pacific Northwest.
- CruisingWorld.com.
- NWYachting.com.
- NWBoatInfo.com.
- PierresBay.com
- SullivanBayMarina.com
- KwatsiBay.com
- LagoonCoveMarina.com

- JennisBay.com
- VancouverIslandNorth.ca

Northern BC's Coast (Inside Passage)

The northern portion of British Columbia becomes much wilder once you leave the Broughtons and head north past Blunden Harbour, Slingsby Channel, and the notorious Cape Caution, where you find yourself unprotected from the Pacific Ocean's weather, waves, and currents. Give yourself plenty of time to wait out poor weather forecasts when traveling beyond Cape Caution and back. Read and heed *Waggoner Cruising Guide* directions for crossing this water. I've done it several times, and if you go when the forecast is fine, you'll probably have an easy trip.

Above Cape Caution, the waters and land are much wilder. Marinas are few, so provision accordingly. The fishing is usually stupendous, and the fjord-like scenery glorious. Since anchorages are fewer and farther from each other, always travel with a Plan A and B, and maybe even C. The northern coast ends where Southeast Alaska begins.

What to enjoy

- Pruth Bay - Hakai Lúxvbális Conservancy and beach. Internet can be found here.
- Provisioning in Shearwater.
- The First Nation town of Bella Bella.
- The ghost town in Ocean Falls.
- Fiordland.
- Look for spirit bears on Princess Royal Island, especially in Buttedale.
- Prince Rupert.
- Bella Coola.

- Take BC ferry from Prince Rupert to Haida Gwaii.

What to watch out for
- Logs and log booms.
- Tugs and barges, commercial and cruise ships.
- Whales.
- Commercial and native fishing.
- Wind against current.
- Strong currents in Hiekish Narrows.
- Lowe Inlet, Verney Falls.

Helpful publications
- *Waggoner Cruising Guide.*
- *Northwest Boat Travel.*
- *Exploring the North Coast of British Columbia.*
- *Proven Cruising Routes, Vol. 1 - Seattle to Ketchikan.*
- *Inside Passage - North Portion* (chart).
- *Inside Passage - South Portion* (chart).
- *Exploring Alaska and British Columbia,* Hilson.
- Fine Edge's *Ports and Passes.*

Internet resources
- ActiveCaptain.com.
- Shearwater.ca.
- Ccrd-bc.ca > Communities.
- BellaCoola.ca.
- Hakai.org > Where We Work.
- OceanFalls.ca.
- SpiritBear.com.
- WaggonerGuide.com, Updates
- BoatTravel.com, Ch. 19.

- NWCruising.net.
- PassageMaker.com, Pacific Northwest.
- CruisingWorld.com.
- NWYachting.com.
- NWBoatInfo.com.

Southeast Alaska

Southeast Alaska begins where you cross the imaginary line in Dixon Entrance that separates Canada from the United States. As when you crossed Cape Caution, when you cross Dixon Entrance into Alaska, the waters and lands become even bigger and wilder. But that's the thrill of it. You'll be enjoying waters and scenery all the way up to Glacier Bay and Skagway. Nature, in all its abundance, will be at your doorstep. Enjoy!

What to enjoy

- All the major towns: Ketchikan, Wrangell, Petersburg, Juneau, Skagway, Sitka, and Hoonah.
- The glaciers in Glacier Bay, Endicot and Tracey Arms, and Dawes.
- Fishing, crabbing, prawning.
- First-Nation villages of Angoon, Craig, Haines, Hoonah, Hydaburg, Kake, and Metlakatla.
- Baronof Warm Springs

What to watch out for

- Whales and other wildlife.
- Commercial and native fishing operations, nets and traps.
- Logs, dead heads, and log booms.
- Ferries and cruise ships.

- Wind against current.
- Time change; Alaska is an hour ahead of BC.
- Adverse weather patterns.
- Ice burgs (burgie bits).

Helpful publications

- *Northwest Boat Travel.*
- *Exploring Alaska and British Columbia* Stephen E. Hilson, Ed.
- *Exploring Southeast Alaska,* Don Douglass and Réanne Hemingway-Douglass.
- SE Alaska Tides and Current publications.

Internet resources

- ActiveCaptain.com.
- TravelJuneau.com.
- Visit-Ketchikan.com.
- Sitka.org.
- Skagway.com.
- PetersburgAlaska.com
- TravelJuneau.com
- WaggonerGuide.com, Updates.
- BoatTravel.com, Chapter 20.
- NWCruising.net.
- PassageMaker.com, Pacific Northwest.
- CruisingWorld.com.
- NWYachting.com.
- NWBoatInfo.com.

Chapter Four

Planning Your Cruise

Sharing and Organizing the Responsibilities

The Boat Notebook ★ List of Common Cruising Tasks

Cruising is a lot of fun, and a lot of work. I like to call it fun work, which most of it is. When it doesn't seem so fun, I call it the Joys of Cruising.

It might not seem obvious, but before you go cruising in the PNW, you really need to think about how your and the Captain's responsibilities are divided up. In fact, I'll bet if you get this part of your cruise started off on the right foot, your cruise will be considerably easier.

As *L'Esprit*'s First Mate, I'm motivated by three goals that I think will make all our cruising experiences, short or long distance, more satisfying. I want the Captain and me to:

- Have jobs we're capable of, even if they take us out of our comfort zones a bit.
- Trust the other is focused on and accomplishing his/her job, so we're not distracted from our own.

- Be aware of the other's responsibilities so if something happens to one of us, the other can take over.

To meet these three goals on L'*Esprit*, I created a list of all the tasks necessary to complete the usual events, like docking, navigating, etc. Obviously, this list gets tweaked from time to time. Then Capt. Dave and I agreed on who accomplishes what. This also changes from time to time.

After I compiled the initial list, I went through the list of my tasks and asked myself two questions:

- What additional information and training, if any, will help me best accomplish this task?
- If something were to happen to Dave, what information and training do I need to accomplish his tasks?

The Boat Notebook

Answering these questions motivated me to create a Boat Notebook in which I keep step-by-step instructions for turning on and off the water maker, the engines, the generator, and the dinghy engine. The Boat Notebook contains scripts to use when talking to the Coast Guard, another boat or ship, and marinas, as well as scripts to use when talking with customs. I've got a drawings of how the electrical panel should look while we're underway, we're anchored, or at a marina with electricity.

The Boat Notebook contains a diagram illustrating where all L'*Esprit*'s drawers, closets, nooks, and crannies are located. Corresponding to this diagram, there are lists showing where everything is stored, because believe me, it's easy to forget where you put the bug spray or the sewing kit or the batteries for the electronic thermometer. Plus, if something were to happen to me, these lists would help Capt. Dave find his beloved Alaskan Amber, Snickers, and granola bars. The Boat Notebook also has recipes, including recipes for packaged food because, as you'll read later, you want to get rid of as much packaging as possible.

Is it necessary for you list all these mechanical steps and provisioning locations? Yes. Maybe not in such detail if you're chartering. But yes, it's necessary. Remember, ignorance is not bliss.

Do you have to keep information in notebook? No. Use folders in a file box. Or use your computer. Lots of cruisers keep their galley and cabin information in Excel files or Word documents. Whatever works best for you. Just remember that easy access is important for you and the Captain.

And here I have to admit to you that my Boat Notebook got so full I had to actually separate my galley information from the rest of my boat information. Now I have a Boat Notebook and a Galley Book. You might need to do this too.

List of Common Cruising Tasks

To give you a better picture of breaking down boat events into tasks, look at the following list of normal cruising events that could happen on any given day. You'll see that for each to happen, numerous smaller steps have to be completed by one or both of you.

NOTE: Please don't let this list horrify you, especially if you're new to cruising. All of the tasks and sub-tasks below are covered in this book. Give yourself ample time to become proficient. When you're out cruising, talk with other recreational mariners and seek out their advice. Don't be surprised if everyone wants to help you!

Preparing the boat for departure

- Check the engine oil, antifreeze, and belts, fluid levels, and sea strainers.
- Check the engine area for leaks or unexpected debris.
- Furnish the driving station with all necessary books, binoculars, radios, ferry schedules, and navigation devices.
- Have an agreed-upon destination in mind; also have a Plan B.
- Stow all items which might move around underway.
- Make sure hatches and ports are shut tight.
- Check weather for signs of safe or dangerous passage. (Ch. 20)
- Check charts for obstacles and safe havens in case of emergency.
- Check currents for times of turns, speeds, and directions, (Ch. 18)
- Check depth sounder.
- Pay marina if you're in one.
- Remove and stow canvas, if necessary.

Starting the boat

- Make sure transmission(s) are in neutral.
- Start engine(s) and check for engine water flushing from boat.
- Adjust electric panel.

- Turn on and adjust navigation and communication devices.
- Unplug from shore power and stow cord.

Leaving the dock

- Make lines ready for easy departure.
- Undo lines from dock or boat.
- Stow lines and fenders.
- Check for obstacles and other boats before leaving.

Docking

- Call the marina and obtain a slip assignment.
- Check chart so you know where you're going.
- Check current, wind direction, and depth sounder.
- Prepare lines and fenders for landing.
- Drive boat to slip or dock.
- Step from boat to dock and secure the lines on cleats or bull rails (don't leap).
- Plug in electrical cord, if there is one.
- Adjust electrical panel.
- Turn off radios and navigation equipment and stow.
- Sign in at the marina, if visiting.

Anchoring

- Check chart for best places to anchor. (Ch. 21)
- Check current, wind direction, and depth sounder.
- Calculate high and low tide depths.
- Prepare anchor for dropping.
- Note the direction other boats are facing and face that way.

- Drop anchor and let out the correct amount of scope to accommodate highest tide depth.
- Give anchor and chain a few moments to settle.
- Back down.
- Rig bridle or snubber.
- Keep anchor watch and report on findings.

Shutting down the boat
- State that you're going to shut down the engines.
- Shut down engine(s).
- Clean up driving station and stow all books and devices.
- Plug into electricity if using marina electricity.
- Adjust electrical panel.
- Re-cover with canvas, if needed.
- Enter trip data in log book.

Dinghy
- Get it off the boat and into the water OR if you tow it, bring it up to the big boat so you can get into it.
- Load all required equipment: oars, bailer, registration information, life vests for everyone aboard, whistle, navigation lights, and for Canada, you also need a boarding device and a heaving line that floats.
- Load personal GPS, marine or family radios, and grapnel anchor if you desire.
- Start engine or put oars in locks and tour.
- Before leaving anchorage, put dinghy back on boat or secure tow line.

Going through customs

- Gather passports, driver's licenses.
- Gather lists of boat registration numbers, Nexus or CanPass numbers if you have them
- Create list of items to declare.
- Gather credit card in case customs requires you to pay duty on an item.
- Gather phone numbers for US Customs in Washington and/or Alaska and for Canadian Customs (see *Waggoner* Guide).
- Estimate time of arrival at customs station.
- Gather customs script if you're not feeling confident.
- Gather paper to write on.
- If you have Nexus, gather cell phone and ear buds so you can hear over engine noise when contacting customs.

Having a meal

- If you have an all electric galley, you may need to turn on generator to use stove, oven, or microwave.
- If you have a gas galley, open the tank valve, and then turn on the solenoid breaker.
- Figure out how to make what you are having with the fewest pans and dishes.
- Figure out how to get refrigerated foods out by opening door as few times as possible.
- Cook or prepare your meal.
- Deal with garbage.
- To clean up afterward, you'll need to turn on the water pressure.

- Wash up the dishes and let them air dry OR dry with towel.
- Put dishes away.

Provisioning in a port

- Check on-going list of what needs resupplying for galley, personal care, and boat requirements (i.e., fuel, antifreeze, filters, etc.).
- Clean out refrigerator or reefer.
- Create master list.
- Gather cart, shopping bags, credit card.
- Walk, take taxi, or ride bike to grocery, liquor, and hardware store (or facsimile)
- When back at the boat, stow the receipts.
- Stow food by: removing excess packaging, vacuum sealing if you like, labeling, and adding purchases to list of stocked boat items.
- Get rid of trash before departing the dock if possible. Otherwise stow trash for later removal.

Doing laundry in a port

- Gather at least twenty dollars or loonies in change (except for Broughtons marinas where laundry becomes part of your entire bill).
- Gather detergent, softener, cart and bags of laundry (or however you do it).
- Bring something to read.
- De-lint the dryer screen often to facilitate drying.

Engine maintenance while cruising

- Have a list showing what all fluid levels should be in Boat Notebook.

- Have a list of all specific products used on your boat in Boat Notebook.
- Have on board an up-to-date maintenance log for your boat and dinghy in Captain's Log book.
- Have the phone numbers of your favorite boat servicers in Boat Notebook.
- Have on board extra filters, oil and other fluids, gaskets, pumps, impellers, dinghy patches, etc.
- Routinely check: fluid levels; raw water filters; presence or symptoms of leaks; belts; hoses; zincs; batteries; deck and navigation lights; anchor connections; bilge; and lines, sails, and rigging (if sailing).
- If something needs replenishing or fixing, replenish it or fix it.

Heads

- To shower, turn on water pressure at electrical panel. Or use a Sun Shower that's warmed in the sun.
- After showering, pump sump.
- To use toilet, add water before sitting down. If you're only urinating, this is not required.
- Use either marine-grade toilet paper that can be flushed, or use regular paper and toss it in trash. Empty trash often!
- Flush according to the product's directions.
- For your holding tank, use Noflex Digestor according to directions. It's the best in my opinion.

Navigating to a destination

- Refer to at least two charts: one paper and one electronic, or two different electronic charts
- Plot your course and your Plan B.
- Before getting underway, look at charts for all obstacles such as rocks, reefs, shoals, shipping lanes, rapids, narrows, navigation aids (buoys, etc.) and adverse current conditions.
- Follow plotted course, except when it must be changed.

Before you leave home for an extended cruise

- Decide where you want to go.
- Stow the best personal flotation devices you can afford for your body type. Attach a whistle to each one.
- Have on board several life-saving floating devices.
- Have your fire extinguishers checked and certified.
- Top off all fluids, including water and fuel.
- Check all boat batteries; replace if near their retirement age.
- Check water and fuel filters.
- Stow batteries for all other devices: flashlights, GPSs, radios, etc.
- Stow all licenses (including radio licenses), and documentation in the Captain's Log. Stow copies of these in the Boat Notebook.
- Paint or mark your anchor rode in intervals of 30', 60', 90', etc., so you can see how much rode you have out by counting off the markings. The

intervals can be multiples of 25' or 35'. Whatever works for you. Mark your rode to the end.
- Check all sound-producing devices: air horns, boat horns, and hand-held horns.
- Consider having an EPIRB (Emergency Position Indication Radio Beacon.) Register it.
- Replace out-of-date flares.
- Stow a current copy of Waggoner Cruising Guide and Nigel Calder's *Boatowner's Mechanical and Electrical Manual: How to Maintain, Repair, and Improve Your Boat's Essential Systems.*
- Go on the Internet and print World Cruising Wiki's Yacht Maintenance list (cruiserswiki.org > Wiki Contents >Yacht Maintenance). It's more than a checklist. It tells you what to look for, and how to fix it, or it refers you to specific pages of Nigel Calder's book.
- Have your insurance in order; if you're cruising to SE Alaska or BC's northern coast, make certain your insurance allows you to go to your destinations when you plan to go there.
- See doctors and get prescriptions.
- Have your personal communications devices in working order.
- Communicate with your credit card companies so they know where and for how long you'll be travelling.
- Know how you plan on taking care of bills and mail while you're away.
- Have all emergency numbers and information in your Boat Notebook.

- If Canadian, know where and how you can bank in the US, and if American, know the same if you're visiting Canada.
- If needed, establish who is watching your home while you are away.
- Have all photography equipment ready to use.
- Have computers, tablets, Kindles, etc. ready to go.
- Purchase fishing licenses for the countries in which you plan to fish.

This long list is the meat of the First Mate's Guide.

All these tasks need to be divided up and accomplished by the Captain and/or you, the First-Mate.

If you need help with some of your tasks, like going through customs, you'll find the help you need in this book, or you'll be guided to a place where you can get an even better answer.

If you need some help just becoming familiar with some of the Captain's tasks, you'll find that help here too.

The next chapters help you before you ever leave the dock. Then you'll read about being underway.

PREPARING TO CRUISE

Chapter Five

Preparing to Cruise

The Boat Notebook

The things that motivate me before we ever leave home for the wild blue yonder are:

- Having a safe, comfortable, easy trip.
- Coming home to very few surprises

This means I have to foresee a lot of issues and solve them before we leave. I may seem to go a little overboard with some of these things, but that's because we leave for two to three months at a time. If you're only going to be gone for a couple of weeks, there are some things you can definitely skip or go light on.

You're going to be getting a lot of information in this book, in fact too much information. If you don't have a way to organize it, you'll kind of go crazy, which is exactly what I don't want for you.

Thus, I highly suggest that the first thing you do is create your Boat Notebook.

My primary motivators when telling you about the First-Mate's Boat Notebook are to help you:

- Feel you can easily find information you need.
- Feel confident in accomplishing your First Mate tasks, or at least feel confident that you are continually improving in doing those tasks.

Keeping that in mind, I'll give you the directions for compiling your Boat Notebook under the assumption that you'll be using a loose-leaf notebook. If you're using folders stored in a box or files stored on your computer, please feel free to adapt my instructions to suit you.

First, get dividers for at least nine sections.

The sections will be in some order:

- Contacts
- Customs
- Destinations
- Expenses
- Mechanics
- Navigation
- Provisions
- Scripts
- To Dos

Then, over the weeks it will take you to prepare for your cruise, place the pertinent information in each section.

In CONTACTS, place all information regarding people you will need to get hold of in case of emergencies, boat issues, credit card and bank issues, etc.

In the CUSTOMS section, place all information having to do with customs: copies of driver's licenses and passports, lists of duty sensitive products, etc. Keep your prescription information in this section as customs may ask you for it.

In the DESTINATIONS section, place information you've compiled about destinations you plan to visit. Include information such as marina diagrams, city maps, phone numbers, etc. Print out anything you find important to have from ActiveCaptain.com

In the EXPENSES section, keep a running tab of your expenditures so you can compare them with your credit card bill when you get home.

The MECHANICS section is where you keep directions for turning on and off engines, generators, etc. It is where you have a list of default fluid levels and products that need to be repurchased from time to time. I'd advise you keep all you user manuals in a separate notebook or file, otherwise your Boat Notebook will not be able to close. You might also want to include pages you printed out from the World Cruising Wiki's Yacht Maintenance list (CruisersWiki.org > Wiki Contents > Yacht Maintenance).

The NAVIGATION section holds information about the rules of the road, figuring times of slack water, etc.

The PROVISIONS section contains the diagram of all your boat's drawers and cupboards, plus the list of all the items you've stored on the boat and where they are. If you like, keep recipes in this section also.

Note: As I've said before, on *L'Esprit*, I keep my provisioning and food preparation information in my 8.5" x 5.5" Galley Book instead of in the Boat Notebook. If you're going on a long cruise, say a month or more, I'd suggest you keep all your provisioning and galley information in a separate notebook that you keep in the galley. Otherwise your Boat Notebook might become too jam-packed to be practical.

The SCRIPTS section contains scripts for talking on the marine radio and on the telephone to customs. (Ch. 11)

The TO DOS section has checklists of things that have to be done when taking off, coming home, etc.

You may decide you want to divide the information differently, and please feel comfortable doing so. Maybe you only want to use more than two notebooks. And maybe you want to use the smaller binders for 8.5" x 5.5" paper, rather than the regular sized binders for 8.5" x 11" paper. Please feel comfortable to use what works best for you.

But I suggest you don't use a spiral binder because:

- It won't be flexible for all your needs
- You can't add valuable print-outs and pamphlets that you'll end up collecting.

Also, you don't have to put everything I suggest in your notebooks, just as you may find you include some things I don't mention. Again do what works for you. In any case, I'll share with you what motivates me to include certain things in my notebooks in the hopes it will help you too.

What you'll need if organizing using notebooks

- One or more 3-ring binders
- Index tabs
- Notebook paper

Internet Resources

CruisersWiki.org > Wiki Contents > Yacht Maintenance

Chapter Six

Preparing to Cruise

Life-Preserving and Safety Equipment

Personal Floatation Jackets and Vests
Life Rings or Slings and Throw Ropes ★ Epirbs
Flares and Visual Distress Signals ★ Fire Extinguishers
Bells and Whistles ★ Ventilation and Backfire-Flame Arrestor
Other Canadian Safety Requirements

Being out on the water and cruising in the Inside Passage are the very definition of bliss. The water sparkles, and the eagles soar aloft.

But then there's an emergency. Then cruising can be downright frightening. That's why on *L'Esprit*, we make sure all our safety and life-preserving equipment is always up to speed.

The things that always motivate me when it comes to life-preserving equipment are:

- Not losing my husband, my guests, or my own life.

- Reducing the time one of us has to spend in the icy PNW water.
- Satisfying our insurance company's requirements in case we do have an accident or emergency (we want them to honor our claims, if any).

As First Mate, you'll want to make sure your boat has all the personal flotation devices you'll need for your trip. These include jackets or vests, life rings or slings, flotation cushions for your dinghy, throw ropes, and a step-on ladder of some sort.

Personal Floatation Jackets and Vests

Whether you're making a short hop to a neighboring island, or a full scale cruise to SE Alaska, you'll want to have the best life vests you can afford for your body type and preferred activities. There are all sorts of devices to choose from, and you may end up with a couple of kinds. For example, on *L'Esprit*, we have:

- Inflatable life vests and jackets, as well as their re-arming kits, which we wear in the dinghy and when docking.
- Floatation jackets that have buoyant foam sewn into the lining for when Dave goes out on the deck to work the anchor and lines.
- Non-inflatable life vests for when we kayak, since we're more liable to get wet. If we end up in the water, we hang the vests out to dry. This saves on re-arming kits for inflatable vests.

When we have pets or children on board, we make sure there are life vests for them too. Children don't float, and neither do many pets.

Last, check that all life vests and jackets have a whistle attached, and that there is at least one jacket on board per person.

Life Rings or Slings, and Throw Ropes

You'll want to make sure you have at least one life ring or life sling and a throw rope aboard your boat in case someone falls overboard. Be sure it's accessible and has your boat's name on it somewhere.

Practice tossing both the ring or sling and the throw rope a few times so if you have to use them in an emergency you at least have some sense of how they will behave.

Consider Googling "How to toss a life ring," and "How to toss a life sling." You'll find lots of videos and instructive slide shows that illustrate beneficial tossing techniques.

We also keep some floating cushions on board just in case. These cushions are not intended to be used as life-saving devices, so they should never be considered a replacement for life rings or slings. But if someone falls in the water, our plan is to throw them overboard to give them extra aid.

Along with having the proper life-saving equipment on board your boat, you'll want to have Man Overboard Drill directions in your First-Mate's notebook (or folder, or computer file, etc.). Here are some good online resources for you to print or save for your notebook:

- BoatUS.com. In search window enter: man overboard drill June 2012. Print it out. Put it in your Boat Notebook.
- WorkingTheSails.com. In search site window enter: yacht emergency drills.
- PsychoSnail.com. Click on Sailing > Man Overboard Procedure.
- SailingMagazine.net. In search window enter: Crew Overboard Recovery May 2013.

A worthwhile discussion for you and the Captain is how you'll get the person overboard back on the boat. The discussion Capt. Dave and I have had has led us to do the following:

- We've added metal, drop-down steps at the stern of the boat.
- Capt. Dave rigged a clip-and-pulley system with enough purchase for me to lift him out of the water if necessary.
- We've stored about 100 yards of bright yellow floating heaving line with a monkey fist on the end in a soft bag that's attached to our stern rail. The end of the heaving line is also attached to the soft bag so when it's thrown it's still attached to the boat.

EPIRBS

If your budget allows, you might consider buying or renting an Epirb (Emergency Position Indicating Radio Beacon). You register it with the Coast Guard. When it gets set off because you or your boat is in real distress, the Coast

Guard will come find you because they've received your latitude and longitude from your Epirb.

I insisted we have one on board because Capt. Dave sometimes single-hands our boat to the local islands, and I worry his Robinson Crusoe ways can leave him in harm's way.

Flares and Visual Distress Signals

Flairs are important for emergency situations. As First Mate, you'll need to know where they're located on your boat and help make certain they are all less than 42 months old. If the American or Canadian Coast Guard boards you and discovers your flares are old, they can write you up and fine you.

When you are in American waters, US Coast Guard requires you to have at least:

- Boats less than 16': between sunset and sunrise, one electric distress light OR three combination day/night red flares.
- Boats longer than 16': One hand-held meteor or parachute flare, and one of the following combinations: One electric distress light and one orange distress flag OR three floating or hand-held orange smoke signals and one electric distress light OR three combination day/night flares.

When you are in Canadian waters, the Canadian Coast Guard requires you to have at least:

- Boats between 5.5 to 8 meters: three A, B, or C type flares and three A, B, C, or D type flares, for a total of six.

- Boats between 8 to 20 meters: six A, B, or C type flares and six A, B, C, or D type flares, for a total of twelve.

Fire Extinguishers

You're required by both the American and Canadian Coast Guards to have up-to-date and certified fire extinguishers on board your boat.

The US Coast Guard requires you to have at least:

- Non-commercial boats up to 26' with inboard engine: One B-1 type Coast Guard-approved hand portable fire extinguisher.
- Boats between 26' and 40': Two B-1 type approved portable fire extinguishers OR one B-2 type.
- Boats between 40' and 65': Three B-1 type approved portable fire extinguishers OR one B-1 type and one B-2 type.

The Canadian Coast Guard requires you to have at least:

- Boats up to 8 meters that have inboard engine and a gas or liquid stove: One Class B-I fire extinguisher.
- Boats 8 to 12 meters that have inboard engine and a gas or liquid stove: One Class B-II fire extinguisher.
- Boats 12 to 20 meters: Two Class B-II fire extinguishers (one by sleeping cabin entrances and one at entrance to engine); One Class B-II fire extinguisher if boat uses gas or liquid to cook or heat.

Bells and Whistles

The US and Canadian Coast Guards require you to have sound-making devices on your vessel, dinghy, and life vest. These devices range from whistles to clanging bells, loud hailers, and horns.

The US Coast Guard requires:

- Boats up to 39.4' need to have one effective noise device.
- Boats longer than 39.4' need to have two effective noise devices.

The Canadian Coast Guard requires:

- Boats up to 18' must have whistles attached to life vests. This includes your dinghy.
- Boats from 18' to 26' must have one sound-making device
- Boats over 26' but less than 100' must have a whistle and a bell.

Ventilation and Backfire-Flame Arrestor

If your boat uses gasoline for propulsion or to run its generator, be sure that her backfire flame arrestor and ventilation ducts are up to code for her length and type and are functioning properly.

For more information about the U.S. Coast Guard's federal requirements for recreational boats, visit USCGBoating.org. Be sure to look up your state's regulations, or the state you'll be visiting, since often state regulations are more rigorous than federal ones.

Other Canadian Safety Requirements

If you'll be cruising to or through Canadian waters, check with the Canadian Coast Guard's Office of Boating Safety. Some boats require you to carry a fire axe, water buckets, a manual bilge pump, and a hand bailer.

Personally, I think you'd want to carry them whether they're required or not.

Other Safety Gear

Though not required, consider having jack lines and tethers on board for times when a crew members needs to go on deck in rough weather during a passage. A jack line is attached to the boat's bow and is then drawn to the back of the boat, where it is attached. All parts of a jack line should be inboard of the stanchions. One end of a tether attaches to the crew member's life vest, and the other end is attached to the jack line in such a way that it can move with the crew member's movements fore and aft. If the crew member falls overboard, he is still attached to the boat.

Likewise, consider making up lanyards to keep things from falling overboard. Tie one end of lanyard to the boat, and tie the other end to the item you don't want accidentally lose overboard. Lots of times we tie lanyards around our neck and attach items to the lanyard, like Chapstick, magnifying glasses, etc.

For Your Boat Notebook

- A check-off list of all your safety equipment, including the last date each was inspected and/or replaced.

- Directions for preferred Man-over-Board procedure
- Directions for using fire extinguisher.
- Directions for using the loud hailer and fog horn.

Chapter Seven

Preparing to Cruise

Sound and Light-Producing Devices

Sound-Producing Devices ★ Light-Producing Devices

Like flotation vests and life slings, which are considered life-preserving devices, I think of sound and light-producing devices as boat-preserving devices. They make your boat noticeable to all the other boats and ships around you.

As First Mate, the things that always motivate me when it comes to sound- and light-producing devices are:

- Being seen and heard by other boats at anchor, in weather, and when entering and leaving blind turns.
- Alerting other boats of our intentions.
- Being able to communicate with other boats and the Coast Guard.
- Satisfying our insurance company's requirements in case we do have an accident or emergency (we want them to honor our claims, if any).

Okay, well maybe you don't have to do this each time you leave home, but at the beginning of the cruising season, then occasionally during the season, and of course before leaving on a long cruise, take time to check that the following safety devices on your boat work as you expect:

Sound-Producing Devices

Air horns, boat horns, and hand-held horns

Your boat neighbors might not love you for testing all your horns, but they'll eventually get over it, or they'll feel inspired to blast theirs.

Ship-to-ship radios

Checking your marine radio is an important practice because if you're putting out a distress signal that no one can hear, well, you're sunk. But doing these checks annoys the heck out of other boaters. You have to tune your radio to a frequently used channel and say, "This is OurBoat, OurBoat, requesting a radio check."

Hopefully someone will reply that they hear you. OR you can use SeaTow's Automated Radio Check Service (ARCS) by tuning into VHF Channel 24, 25, 26, 27, 28, or 84 (whichever works best), and say, "This is OurBoat, OurBoat, requesting a radio check."

When you release the mike, SeaTow's system replays your transmission, which lets you know what others hear.

In addition to making sure your equipment works, check that your Boat Notebook contains emergency marine radio scripts for you or your guests to use, as well as information describing what sounds and signals mean. You'll read more about this while you're under way.

What the horn blasts mean

Horn blasts aren't used a lot by cruisers, but they are important to understand. Even if you never blast your horn, ships and tugs around you definitely will. You'll want to know what their horn signal means so you can respond if necessary.

1 short blast means the ship wants to pass the other boat down ship's port side.

2 short blasts mean the ship wants to pass the other boat down the ship's starboard side.

3 short blasts tell everyone the ship is backing up.

5 short blasts mean danger because the ship doesn't understand the other boat's intentions and wants to make sure everyone will be safe.

1 long blast means the ship is entering or leaving a blind turn, or it's near an obstructed area, or its leaving its dock or anchorage.

1 long blast every two minutes is the ship's fog horn which it uses when there's low visibility.

Light-Producing Devices

Running lights

Test when you can see them shine, like after sunset or before sunrise. Lights should be visible from at least 2 nm away (3 nm for boats longer than 39.4', 5 nm for boats longer than 65.7', and 1 nm for boats 16' or shorter).

Anchor lights

Again, test between sundown and sunup. You want other boats to see you from at least 2 nm away (3 nm for boats longer than 39.4', 5 nm for boats longer than 65.7', and 1 nm for boats 16' or shorter).

Flashlights and handheld navigation lights

Be sure you have plenty of batteries and/or battery chargers, as well as replacement bulbs.

What the lights mean

On all vessels, the red light indicates the port side. Think of red as being port wine! Obviously, then, the green light is on the right or starboard side.

With that in mind, if you see:

- GREEN on left, RED on right, it means the vessel is coming toward you.
- RED on left, GREEN on right, it means the vessel is going away from you.
- If you only see a RED light, the vessel is moving from your right to left.
- If you only see a GREEN light, the vessel is moving from your left to right.

Also be aware of the stacks of lights on working vessels.

Two WHITE lights mean the other vessel is a towing vessel.

For more information, visit USCGBoating.org, *US Aids to Navigation System: What You Need to Know about the Markers on the Water*.

For Your Boat Notebook

- A check-off list of all your sound- and light-producing devices, including the last date each was inspected and/or replaced.

- Print outs of marine radio protocol, etiquette, and scripts (Ch. 11); marine radio stations in Washington, British Columbia, and Alaska; marine horn signals; and marine light signals.

Resources

- USCGBoating.org, "US Aids to Navigation System: What You Need to Know About the Markers on the Water."
- WestMarine.com. Navigation Light Rules.

Chapter Eight

Preparing to Cruise

The Boat Library

Navigating Safely ★ Finding Safe Harbors and Anchorages
Discovering and Repairing Boat Issues
Eating Well and Staying Healthy

Your boat's library is the where you retrieve information about anything you might need while in or near a port and out in the middle of nowhere. This library can contain information printed in books or saved on your computer, iPad, Kindle, tablet, and/or phone.

What motivates me when I appraise *L'Esprit*'s library is my desire to:

- Figure out where we are, where we are going, and how to get there safely.
- Be able to fix and operate things, from the boat engine to the marine radio to the making of our daily meals.

As First Mate, I suggest you have books (paper or electronic) on board that help you:

- Navigate safely.
- Find safe harbors/anchorages.
- Discover and repair problems on your boat.
- Eat well and stay healthy.

Safe Navigation

Good resources for safe navigation will give lots of information about the specific waters through which you'll be travelling. These books, computer programs and applications include cruising guides, navigation software, current and tide tables, and charts.

Obviously there are more publications than what I provide here, but we have found these the most useful. Also, this book is published near the end of 2016, so more recent publications won't be listed.

The following are highly recommended publications for cruising in the Inside Passage:

- *Waggoner Cruising Guide*, the most current edition (it's published every year by Fine Edge).
- *Northwest Boat Travel*, by Kathy Newman, the most current edition.
- *Ports and Passes*, by Chyna Sea Ventures Ltd.
- Generic and usually-free tides and currents booklet for areas you'll be cruising (Puget Sound, British Columbia, Alaska).
- Anne and Laurence Yeadon-Jones' *Dreamspeaker Cruising Guides* for areas in which you'll be cruising: Puget Sound, San Juan Islands, Gulf and (east) Vancouver Islands, Vancouver through Sunshine Coast, Discovery Islands and Desolation

- Sound, the Broughtons, Vancouver Island's West Coast.
- Don Douglass and Réanne Hemingway-Douglass's *Exploring Series Cruising Guides* for areas you'll be cruising: Puget Sound, San Juan and Gulf Islands, British Columbia's South Coast, British Columbia's North Coast, South-East Alaska, Vancouver Island's West Coast.
- Kevin Monahan & Don Douglass's *Proven Cruising Routes, Vol. 1* - Seattle to Ketchikan.
- Kevin Monahan's *Local Knowledge* — the Skipper's Reference.
- Fine Edge's planning maps for areas you'll be cruising: North Inside Passage, South Inside Passage, San Juan and Gulf islands, Desolation Sound, West and East Prince William Sound.
- Stephen E. Hilson, Ed.'s *Exploring Alaska and British Columbia* and *Exploring Puget Sound and British Columbia*.
- *Marine Atlas Vol. 1: Olympia to Malcolm Island*, and *Marine Atlas Vol. 2: Port Hardy to Skagway*. Vol. 2 is easier to read than Vol. 1, but they're both good books to have available near the helm.
- US Aids to Navigation: *What You Need to Know About the Markers on the Water* and *The Canadian Aids to Navigation System 2011*.
- Weather and Sea Status apps for computer, phone, and tablet: SeaStatus, Predict Wind, NOAA Buoys Live. Marine Weather, Marine Weather (by AccuWeather).

- Navigation software for computer, phone, and tablet: Garmen, Navionics, Nobeltec, Rose Point.

NOTE: Fine Edge publishes many other books and foldouts you will probably find useful. Do yourself a favor and visit their website.

Finding Harbors and Anchorages

Publications for finding safe harbors and anchorages will let you know about surrounding terrain, personal experiences, and pertinent details about specific marinas, bays, and coves.

- David Kutz's *The Burgee*, illustrated book of marinas from Olympia to Port Hardy, B.C.
- Anne Vipond and William Kelly's *Best Anchorages of the Inside Passage* (Gulf Islands to Cape Caution).
- Anne and Laurence Yeadon-Jones' *Dreamspeaker Cruising Guide*s for areas in which you'll be cruising: Puget Sound, San Juan Islands, Gulf and (east) Vancouver Islands, Vancouver through Sunshine Coast, Discovery Islands and Desolation Sound, the Broughtons, Vancouver Island's West Coast.
- Don Douglass and Réanne Hemingway-Douglass's *Exploring Series* Cruising Guides for areas you'll be cruising: Puget Sound, San Juan and Gulf Islands, British Columbia's South Coast, British Columbia's North Coast, South-East Alaska, Vancouver Island's West Coast.

NOTE: Again, Fine Edge publishes many other books and fold-outs you will probably find useful. Do yourself a favor and visit their website.

Discovering and Repairing Boat Issues

The publications for discovering and repairing boat issues include:

- Nigel Calder's *Boatowner's Mechanical and Electrical Manual: How to Maintain, Repair, and Improve Your Boat's Essential Systems.*
- Don Casey's *Complete Illustrated Sailboat Maintenance Manual: Including Inspecting the Aging Sailboat, Sailboat Hull and Deck Repair*
- Internet links to: CruisersWiki.org. Wiki Contents > Yacht Maintenance and to WestMarine.com
- All manuals for your boat's systems and products.

Eating Well and Staying Healthy

Publications for eating well and staying healthy include:

- An all-purpose cookbook such as Mark Bittman's *How to Cook Everything* or Irma S. Rombauer and Marion Rombauer Becker's *Joy of Cooking.*
- General first-aid book such as *DK's First Aid Manual* or Joseph and Amy Alton's *The Survival Medicine Handbook: A Guide for when Help is not on the Way.*

For Your Boat Notebook

- Directions for calculating tides and currents for specific times and places, (Ch. 18).
- Step-by-step instructions for starting and stopping boat engine and generator.
- Marine radio instruction and scripts (Ch. 11).
- List of marine weather stations and telephone numbers. Find in *Waggoner Cruising Guide*.
- Chart illustrating locations of all marine weather reporting stations (buoys, lighthouses, etc.) Find in *Waggoner Cruising Guide*.
- List of marine-radio channels for regions through which you'll be cruising. Find in *Waggoner Cruising Guide*.
- List of emergency phone numbers for areas you'll be cruising, and for your insurance companies, your personal physician, your bank, your credit card companies, and your boat mechanic. Feel free, of course, to include other numbers you think are important to have.

Chapter Nine

Preparing to Cruise

Provisioning the Galley

Minimizing and Dealing with Garbage
Cleaning Up the Galley ★ Staying Healthy
Staying Happy ★ Cooking in a Galley
Provisioning Your Galley in Ten Steps

This is a biggie. If you do a good job figuring out the food for your cruise, you will have made huge strides in making sure you and the crew are healthy, comfortable, and happy. And if you mess this up, well, you'll do better next year!

That's why, when I think of provisioning, I'm motivated by:

- Creating the least amount of garbage.
- Creating the least mess to wash up.
- Staying healthy.
- Staying happy (certain foods or their lack can cause emotional disturbances!).
- Making food that can be made on our boat.

Before I go into the actual steps of provisioning, I'm going to explain the above five bullet points, because understanding them will help you understand the finer points of provisioning.

Minimizing and Dealing with Garbage

As you travel north into through the Inside Passage, there are fewer and fewer places to get rid of garbage. Because of this, you'll want to incorporate, and even invent, ways to minimize your trash. When I first started cruising in the PNW, fellow members of our Fidalgo Yacht Club warned me:

- Get rid of as much packaging as possible before you leave.
- Use a compost pail to separate wet trash from dry.
- If you burn trash on a remote beach, do so on an in-coming tide (you can't always do this because of burn bans during dry summers).

Cleaning Up the Galley

When you're cruising, fresh water on your boat is a finite and cherished commodity. Even if you have a water maker on board, water is a finite commodity.

Therefore, when you prepare meals, you'll want to create as little wash-up mess as possible. This means you'll make more one-pot or one-pan meals than you normally do at home. Or you'll learn to keep things warm as you cook three different items in one pan. You'll grill oftener, except if the weather's sloppy, which it normally is in late spring.

As you can see, cooking aboard requires a certain amount of creativity on your part, especially if you don't want to run out of water.

Staying Healthy

This is easy. Keep everything clean. Keep perishables cold. Vacuum the air out of food bags to prevent decay. Eat as many vegetables as you can, even if that means rehydrating them. Eat four or five different food colors at every meal. If you do these things, you'll probably be fine over the long haul.

Staying Happy

This is a two-fold topic.

First, I think everyone on board should have plenty of their favorite comfort foods, and they should know where to find that food in the middle of the darkest night.

On *L'Esprit* that means we have a dedicated chocolate drawer because one of my life mottos is: "Let's have some chocolate and then we can talk about this problem we're having. We also have too many bags of potato chips in the v-berth.

From reading this, you might think we sit around eating chocolate and chips.

We don't.

But sometimes, when the weather's been too awful or a problem has arisen on the boat, our mood and ability to cope sometimes devolve. On those occasions we've learned that having a little of our favorite comfort foods gives our brains the chemicals they need to life our mood and help us think more clearly. Note: There can be a variety of comfort foods.

Second, if you and the Captain get a bit grouchy with each other, it could be because your blood sugar is low, and you could both use a little something healthy to eat. Sometimes people eat less when they're cruising, for one reason or another. Maybe they forget to eat. Or no one wants to go below to prepare food while underway.

Have healthy snacks, like trail mix, aboard for times like these.

Cooking in a Galley

I've owned several boats, and I've been on hundreds of other boats, and here's what I know: Not all boats and boat galleys are alike.

The foods that are easy to prepare and serve on one boat are not necessarily going to be easy to prepare and serve on another.

Some boats are all electric, and foods are routinely pre-cooked, frozen, and then reheated in a microwave. They do this because often the generator has to be on in order to cook.

Other boats cook with propane or alcohol. So they don't need to turn on a generator to cook.

Lots of boats depend on the grill they attach to their exterior stanchions.

Some boats have full blown refrigerators and freezers, while others have reefers (ice-boxes).

Some cruisers love to use their microwave, while some don't (that's me—I had mine removed).

So before you even start thinking about provisioning, figure out what can be prepared and served on your boat, and how does the main chef aboard prefer to cook.

Note: Induction burners are growing in popularity with boaters because they use less electricity. Keep in mind you'll need special pots and pans to use these burners.

Provisioning Your Galley in Ten Steps

If you're planning to cruise longer than two weeks, and especially to remote areas, I suggest you follow these steps chronologically, at least the first time you provision.

First, know your comfort foods

At least a month before your departure, preferably two, make a list of easy-to-grab comfort foods for you and the Captain and anyone else who will be on board with you. There should be at least three types of items per individual, and you can trust this list because you've actually asked the people who will be consuming the food.

Second, think ease of preparation

Make a list of foods you both or all like to eat that can be easily prepared on your boat. This is actually a tricky question because it requires you to think about:

- Having the ingredients on board (storage, trash, etc.).
- Preparing it without creating too much wash-up mess.
- Preparing it with the equipment you have or will have on board.
- Serving it.
- Cleaning up afterwards.

Going through this little exercise you might realize that what you eat onboard may be quite different from what you eat at home. As I mentioned before, I have friends who have natural gas cooking at home but have electric galleys that require their generator be turned on whenever they cook. They tell me they prepare foods at home, freeze them, and then reheat them in the microwave. I have a propane galley, so I'm always making things from scratch.

Your job now is to figure out what you all like to eat and if it can be prepared on board or outside on the boat's grill.

Your list of foods you like will work even better for you if it includes foods that store well without refrigeration. You can find these foods if you do an Internet search. To give you an idea, a short list would include:

- Beans.
- Rice.
- Pasta.
- Potatoes.
- Tortillas.
- Canned foods, including meat and fish.
- Boxed soups.

Third, gather recipes and ideas

Start going through your cookbooks and online cooking sites to find ideas you might want to use. Here are some tips:

- Find recipes that you can alter with different ingredients, like tacos and quesadillas, which you can fill with chicken, beef, or pork, as well as any fish you catch. (I love crab tacos.)

- Visit the FOOD section of Carolyn Shearlock's TheBoatGalley.com and on Pinterest for ideas.
- Download some of FineCooking.com's Create Your Own Recipe Makers. These recipes give you the ratios of whatever ingredients you have to make a risotto, a stew, potato or pasta salad, and pizza, etc.
- Google "one-pan meals" and "one-pot meals."
- The New York Times has a great recipe for No-Knead Bread that uses a cast-iron post with a lid. You can find the recipe on the Internet.
- Do an internet search for Boys Scout and Girl Scout camping recipes. You'll find great one-pot meals, such as their Zip-Lock Omelets.
- If you're really a gourmand, consider adding Karen Page's *The Flavor Bible* to your boat's library. It's a lexicon of what foods and flavors that go best with each other. Out in the wild, it's a real soul saver.
- Use the WonderBag concept, but use fleece. I call it cooking with fleece! Bring rice, beans, lentils, etc. to a boil for five minutes in a lidded, not-too-large cast iron or Le Creuset pot, then wrap it in four or five layers of fleece, and put aside for several hours. When you come back, voila, dinner's ready. I use it regularly for rice on the boat. It takes an hour, and the rice never burns the pot. Experiment at home before trying it on the boat.

Fourth, list ingredients you'll need

Start listing the ingredients you'll need to make all these foods. Consider:

- Using ingredients that can be used in several different dishes.
- Using dehydrated products as ingredients to mix into dishes (milk, eggs, onions, carrots, potatoes, mashed potatoes, tomatoes, mushrooms, and even red wine) No one really likes powdered eggs, but no one can tell the difference if powdered eggs are used to make cookies.
- That rubs can be used in marinades and in sauces for extraordinary flavor enhancement. For grilling, make a concoction of olive oil, a little white or red balsamic vinegar, Dijon mustard and a scoop of your favorite rub. You'll see what I mean.
- Buying Trio sauces in bulk from Amazon or from a Cash & Carry: white sauce, brown sauce, alfredo, cheese sauce, etc. Le Gout has a great cream soup base to which you can just add sautéed vegetables and leftover meat. Buy seasonings too, like for tacos.
- Bringing bouillon in cubes or jars and in various flavors. They add flavor to boring vegetables, among other things.
- Slow-cooking some chicken breasts and pork butt to freeze in meal-size packages and later shred for use in sandwiches, tacos, pastas, wraps, and quesadillas.

- Pre-forming ground meat into patties and freezing in meal-sized batches, whether you'll be using them for burgers or not.

An important question you're probably wondering while reading this is: How much food do I need to bring? First, it's almost impossible to figure this out to a tee, especially if this is your first major cruise or you're new to your boat and the area.

I really hate bringing food back home, but I've gotten used to having to do it. Usually I have too much meat in the freezer because I stress about running out. Sometimes we're lucky and catch a lot of salmon, crab and prawns. When that happens, our freezer stays full because we're not eating the meat I packed.

My rule of thumb is to bring food for one third of a long cruise. My thinking goes like this:

- I'll find stores along the way.
- We'll eat out in towns and marinas.
- We'll be successful hunting and gathering.

At the same time, I factor in the following:

- The area north of Cape Caution to Prince Rupert has only one area where you can find a grocery store, and they're practically on top of each other (Shearwater and New Bella Bella). That's it. If we're travelling in that area, I plan to bring more food.
- The area south of Pender Harbour and Nanaimo to Olympia has many grocery store opportunities, so I'll bring less food.

- The area between Pender Harbour/Nanaimo to Cape Caution has few supermarket opportunities: Comox; Campbell River; Heriot Bay, Quadra Island; Port McNeil; and Port Hardy. There are plenty of small marts, however, that carry limited supplies.
- The high season in Desolation Sound and the Broughtons doesn't really begin until July 1. If we're travelling through this area earlier in the year, I know I can't count on the small marts to carry what I need. So I bring extra butter, flour for making bread if I need it, boxed whipping cream from Trader Joes, etc. Honestly, one year I had to stop at three marinas in the Broughtons to find butter. Another year my only choice was to bake bread; good thing I had a copy of Mark Bittman's *How to Cook Everything* on my Kindle, a book that has saved my sanity more than once.
- The supermarkets in Washington, British Columbia, and Alaska have just about everything you could possibly want. In British Columbia and Alaska, alcohol is sold in a store separate from the market.

Fifth, gather your tools

Create a list of tools you'll need in your galley to prepare the foods you'll be making. If you have a small galley, you'll want to constantly think of ways to save space. Here're some things you'll want to consider:

- Visiting the GEAR sections of Carolyn Shearlock's TheBoatGalley.com and on Pinterest for lots of ideas and product testing.
- Installing magnetic knife holder on your bulkhead, so you have more drawer space.
- Speaking of knives, have a good sharpener on board. A dull knife is a dangerous thing.
- Using a utensil jar on your countertop for spatulas and spoons, in case your drawer space is less than desired.
- Having collapsible products on board: measuring cups, bowls, dish pans, strainers, buckets, etc.
- Buying side-handled pots and pans, rather than those with one long handle. They store better in less space.
- Buying pots and pans with removable handles. Most boating stores carry these.
- Using silicone lids, rather than metal ones, because they're easier to store and take less room. (Thank you, my friend Annette!)
- Having a Soda Stream maker on board so you can make soda as needed, rather than storing all those cans. There are some that take very little space. Don't forget to have plenty of CO_2 canisters.
- Buying some Extra-Life Produce Saver Disks from Amazon. I have found they help fruits and vegetables last longer in my boat's refrigerator.
- Many cruisers love having an electric or stove-top pressure cooker on board. You might consider this for yourself.
- Consider bringing a bread machine on board, especially if you're travelling north of Desolation

- Sound. Bread machines do take up space and use electricity. Zojirushi makes a compact maker that delivers a one-pound loaf.
- Having one of those little computer keyboard vacuum cleaners like the one Veemon sells on Amazon. Here's why: your bread, cheese, and vegetables will last much longer if air is sucked out of the bag in which they're stored. You could, of course, use a straw to suck out the air, but that's not good for your lungs. If you use the little vacuum, you get the same results, but without making yourself sick. This also helps to reduce the need for having an on-board garden.
- Purchasing disposable newborn diapers at the Dollar Store. (I tell you, you're going to love me for this suggestion!) Disposable diapers, when turned inside out and put in your boat's freezer, will significantly reduce frost build-up. That's because the diapers absorb moisture. In fact, I put disposable diapers inside my galley cupboards and lots of other places on the boat to keep things extra dry.
- If saving on electrical use is important, consider having an induction hot plate in your galley. It will need its own pot or pan. See the manufacturer's instructions.

Sixth, set up your notebook

Create a place for recipes in the Provisions section of your notebook. Or, as I mentioned earlier, keep all your provisioning information in a Galley Notebook. I had to do this because I need more room than the Boat Notebook could provide. You may need to do this also.

If you choose to have a separate Galley Notebook, it works to have four sections: Recipes, Appliance Manuals, Provisions Locator, and On-Going Shopping List. It also contains blank paper for you to write lists.

The Recipes section contains:

- Directions from packaging you've removed: cake and cookie mixes, jello and puddings, dehydrated soups, etc. Add recipes whenever you remove packaging.
- Recipes you'll want to make, including the Create-You-Own recipes you find on the Internet.

The Manuals section obviously contains manuals for the food processor, the Soda Stream, the stove, the refrigerator, etc.

The Provisions Locator section holds the diagram showing all the possible places to stow provisions on your boat, as well as the long list of items you've brought on board and stowed, and where you stored them.

The Shopping List section is where you keep track of what you need to buy at the store whenever you find it.

Again, depending on the length and destination of your cruise, the amount of things you have in your galley, and the number of provisions you've stowed, you can keep all this information in the Boat Notebook or in a separate Galley Notebook. Your choice!

Seventh, gather and prepare the food

Make your grocery list, shop, and prepare the food. I'd suggest you empty as much as you can from your home refrigerator and freezer before shopping. When you come home from the store, you'll need cooling space to put the goods.

I'd also suggest that you make peace with the fact that your home kitchen is going to be a bit of smash while you're getting food ready to stow on board. You can ease this by doing a lot of the shopping several weeks ahead of time. That's why in the first step I suggested you begin your provisioning process really more than a month ahead of time.

Here are my suggestions for shopping:

- If you're going to precook any meats or meals, buy those ingredients and cook them up at least a week ahead of time, and store them in your home freezer after vacuum-sealing and labeling.
- If you're dehydrating vegetables, buy those ingredients and start the dehydrating process at least two weeks ahead of departure. You can dehydrate in an oven on low heat or use a dehydrator. Dehydrating takes a surprisingly long time, so remember to account for that. Vacuum seal the dehydrated vegetables or put them in ziplock bags, and label as you complete dehydrating each fruit or vegetable. I typically dehydrate mushrooms, carrots, onions, and parsnips for soups and other one-pot meals. (Note: My friend Kim swears by dehydrating frozen mixed vegetables.)
- If you're planning on having an onboard garden for herbs and vegetables, accommodate for the fact

that the US and Canada do not let you import fresh plants from one country to the next.
- For products you have removed cardboard packaging from, save the directions or ratio-to-water information to put in the Recipes section of your notebook. In most cases, you'll want to save the inner bag, which you'll need to label.
- Consider dividing up frozen vegetables and repackaging them.
- Somewhere in your house have Trader Joe bags or easy-to-carry cartons ready to store room-temperature foods as you're ready them to put on board. Keep like things together as much as possible. Transferring provisions from your home to your boat is an art in itself.
- Bring provisions to your boat during high tides. The gangway will be less steep.

Before bringing provisions to your boat, have an informal running-list of all the things you have prepared for your trip. As you store things in the refrigerator and freezer and in bags/cartons in preparation for taking them to your boat, add each item to that list. This way you can cross-check to make sure you really have what you think you have.

Also before bringing provisions to your boat, decide on a method to keep track of what you have and where it is. There are a couple of ways to keep track of provisions in your notebook.

One way is to have a separate page for each drawer or cupboard or below-decks area. As you add items to each area, just list them on their appropriate page. For example:

Cupboard #3 has 12 cans of tuna, 4 lbs. ground French Roast coffee, etc.

A second way is to just list all your items and indicate where they are next to them. For example, 12 cans of tuna, cupboard #3.

Or you may have another method in mind. Whatever you do, think it through before you go to the boat. Then be consistent with the method you've chosen. You'll thank yourself!

Eighth, prepare your storage plan

Before you store your provisions on your boat, figure out where you're going to put everything, which will probably take a couple of First-Mate/Captain discussions. What you'll both find is that there are two groups of things on your boat which are equally important: the boat tools and fluids, and the cooking tools and food. The problem is that each takes up a lot of space.

Be realistic and creative when you divide up the available space.

Food can be kept in all kinds of places on the boat, just as tools and fluids can. On *L'Esprit*, one drawer in her galley has a bunch of Capt. Dave's tools because he needs quick access to them often. But I also store food on one shelf of a cupboard filled mostly with fuel additives, impellers, and engine manuals. For products stored below decks, I pack them in insulated zippered grocery bags. They're that silvery insulation color on the inside. They have handles which makes it easy to lift them up and drop them back down. And they're a little padded, so the contents experience soft landings.

Once you've allotted your spaces, stick with it in the beginning.

Be open to making changes after you've lived with your plan for a week or so. Talk frankly about each of your needs and make it your priority to meet both of your needs. Where there's a will, there's a way.

Ninth, create your provisioning map

Create a provisioning map in your notebook. Before you stow one thing on my boat before a cruise:

- Draw a diagram showing all the individual places where you can pack your food.
- Then number each spot on the diagram. If you're using insulated zippered grocery bags to stow goods below decks or baskets, number those too. Don't be surprised if you end up with twenty different places, or more!
- Don't lose this diagram. Consider making copies of it. I keep mine in a transparent plastic protector in the notebook.
- Then, as I described earlier, either: 1) create a page (or tab if you're doing this on Excel) for each number. In other words, if you have twenty different storage spots, you should have twenty different pages (or tabs). Number each page (or tab). OR 2) just list all your provisioned items and put each one's location number next to it.

Tenth, stow your goods on your boat

As you stow each item on your boat, write it down on the page whose number that corresponds place's number on the diagram.

On your cruise, when you use an item up, cross it off the list. When you add new products while on your cruise, add those items to the appropriate pages.

Alternately, if you're keeping one long list, write down each item's location number next to it.

NOTE: You might also want to do this with your tools, fluids, replacement parts, and first aid supplies. It's amazing how you'll forget where things are when on an extended cruise.

For Your Boat or Galley Notebook

Your Boat or Galley Notebook (or Provisions file on computer) should have at least four dedicated sections:

- Recipes
- Appliance Manuals
- Provisions locations
- Grocery list

Resources

- TheBoatGalley.com
- WonderBagWorld.com
- Mark Bittman's *How to Cook Everything*
- The Joy of Cooking
- Pinterest.com

Chapter Ten

Preparing to Cruise

The Safe and Healthy Boat

Keeping Everyone on Board Healthy and Safe
Keeping the Boat Healthy and Safe
Keeping the Environment Healthy and Safe

Practically everything in this book comes down to safety. Because there are myriad ways to get hurt on and around a boat, it's vital that safety and health considerations be part of your everyday thinking.

When I think of safety, my primary motivators are:

- Keeping everyone aboard healthy and safe.
- Keeping the boat healthy and safe.
- Doing my part to help others, including the environment, be healthy and safe.

Keeping Everyone on Board Healthy and Safe

Knowing I've probably mentioned some of these topics in other sections of this book, I'll just give you a list of things I've learned about keeping people aboard healthy and safe.

Medicine

Have on board ample over-the-counter medicines you might need in case of colds, headaches, indigestion, toothaches, cuts, burns, etc.

First-aid kit

Besides the above medicines, either purchase a marine first-aid kit or create your own. First aid kits should include at least an generous supply or bandages in all varieties, blood-clotting pads, antibiotic creams and powders, antiseptic solutions and gels, swabs, burn remedies, hydrocortisone cream, sea sickness tablets, cold sore remedies, sting and bite remedies, scissors, instant hot and cold packs, eye wash, Epipen, vinyl gloves, and a ready splint.

Supplements

If you rely on a water maker, know that you are drinking very pure water. Because this means there are few minerals in the water, consider bringing mineral supplements, especially on a long cruise. In my opinion, it's also important to bring vitamin supplements because they help keep you healthy and help to moderate moods.

Clothing

Have clothing and shoes for weather extremes. Carry detergent on board to keep clothing clean and sanitary. Consider having a bar of Naptha soap on board for cleaning clothes if space is an issue.

Cleaning solutions

Have on hand your favorite products for keeping your boat's interior as germ-free as possible. Label them! (Folex is a great all-purpose stain remover for clothing and carpeting. We always have a gallon on board.)

Trash

Have a trash system that keeps unsanitary trash from being exposed to the air you breathe. We keep trash tightly sealed under the floor hatches until we can get rid of them at a marina. Since this takes up a lot of room, I squeeze trash down as tightly as possible to get rid of excess air, which helps. Don't be surprised if a marina charges you to get rid of your trash. Many marinas have recycle bins, so separating bottles and drink cans can be helpful. Also, if you chop up or grind food scraps, you can pitch them overboard.

Drinking water

Know how and where you plan to get potable drinking water. If you're cruising near the mainland, including Vancouver Island, and near large population centers, you can pretty well trust that the municipal water you're getting at the dock has been treated and it's safe to put in your water tank.

For safety's sake put a teaspoon of bleach in your water tank to help kill germs and algae growth. Also, consider using a common water filter, such as Pur or Brita, or an under-sink system.

If you'll be depending on island water during your cruise, you'll want to carry a .5-micron water filter (that's half a micron) to guard against giardia. Giardia is an intestinal infection one can get from drinking unsanitary water. The filter is attached to the faucet end of your water hose.

Another, but more costly, solution is to have a portable or fully-installed water-maker. If you're considering this, but think you might not have the space for an installed water-maker, consider investing in a portable reverse-osmosis system, like the ones manufactured by Rainman. I have not tried out the Rainman system, but I am extremely happy with our US Watermaker (that's the brand name). For boats with limited space, their owners often carry water-filled jerry cans on deck and/or bladders below deck. If you have limited space, you might consider having a salt-water faucet in your galley to limit your fresh-water use when doing the dishes.

Visual clues

Place small rugs on the floor at the bottom of steps which serve as visual indicators for a change in walking pattern. This is especially helpful for the floor areas that people tend to trip on or trip down.

Binoculars

I suggest that your boat have at least two pairs of binoculars, because if you both have your own pair of binoculars, then you don't have to keep changing them back and forth for each's personal visual needs. This is only a big deal in an emergency when you need visual information quickly.

Four eyes

I really suggest that as often as possible have two sets of eyes on the lookout during passages. The Inside Passage can be riddled with debris, especially during spring tides. It's a lot of work for one person to handle. Either that or you both drive alone for half-hour stints.

Tethers

Jack lines and tethers are especially important on sailboats, when the angle of heel may be such that one can easily fall overboard when going to the bow of the boat. Jack lines are long web cords attached near the bow and stern on each side of the boat. A tether is attached to the life vest you should be wearing and to the webbing. If you fall overboard, you'll still be attached to the boat by way of the jack line you're attached to.

Life-jackets

Have plenty of life jackets and floatation devices on board, and know where they are. It is especially important to wear a life jacket when docking and leaving the dock, when in your dinghy, and when anchoring.

Man-overboard

Besides having the required life rings aboard and knowing how to reach a person who has fallen overboard, have a plan for getting that person aboard. This can include adding items to your boat, such as ladders and hoists.

SOS signals

Epirbs and Gpirbs are signal locating devices. When discharged, they notify the Coast Guard of your location so that you can be found and retrieved. I highly recommend having a registered device on your boat, especially if you are on an extended, wilderness cruise. If you fish, crab, or prawn, take the Epirb or Gpirb with you in your dinghy.

Alcohol

Alcohol and other state-altering substances get in the way of safety. Please, for your sake and the sake of other boaters, avoid these substances while underway.

Ditch bag

It is important to prepare your ditch bag and boat-abandoning procedure before you set out on your cruise. Probably and hopefully you will never have to actually use these precautions. But if you do, the ditch bag should include a handheld radio, a waterproof GPS and batteries, at least one powerful floating flashlight, a fog horn, a whistle, a signal mirror, a strobe and batteries, flares and matches, light sticks, duct tape, nylon cord, safety pins, space blankets, garbage bags, zip-locks bags, candle, lighter, fire starters, utility knife, floating cutting board, scissors, vessel documents, wallets, logbook, note pads and pens, bottled water, energy bars, bright bandanas, soap, small first aid kit, prescriptions, and sunscreen. Tie a lanyard to as many of these objects as you can.

Keeping the Boat Healthy and Safe

Anchor

Tie down the anchor if your bow roller doesn't have a keeper. Keepers deter the anchor from bouncing out of the roller when meeting large ship wakes.

Dinghy

Take precautions to secure your dinghy so it's safe for all weather conditions you may meet on your passage.

Anchor line

Make sure you have plenty of scope on your anchor for the size and weight of your boat. If you're planning a trip to SE Alaska, consider having more than three-hundred feet because you may find yourself having to anchor in ninety-feet of water.

Keep your anchor and rode clean. If you've crossed a tall wake or have been in snarly seas, check to make sure your anchor rode didn't become a snarled mess in the chain locker. That can sometimes happen, and it can inhibit smooth anchoring.

Fluid levels

If you plan to make a passage using your engine(s), check the fluid levels, filters, and signs of leaks before departing. Add fluids when needed. Keep on top of cleaning and changing filters. During the summer months grasses and moon jellyfish thrive in the Inside Passage waters; these can clog your filters very quickly.

If you're planning to travel a long distance and that will put more than a hundred hours on your engine, be prepared for having to change your engine oil during that trip. Either that or have someone in mind to change your oil at one of the marinas you plan to visit.

Maintenance schedule

I highly recommend that the Captain create a schedule for maintaining your boat. This schedule should include the boat's engine, plumbing, electrical system, and exterior. If your browse the Internet, you'll find many examples of such schedules. As I've mentioned before, CruisersWiki.org > Wiki Contents > Yacht Maintenance gives a pretty good run down of what needs to be checked regularly and what needs to be checked annually. Give them a peek.

Deck

Regardless of whether you're a sailboat or powerboat, make a routine deck check before leaving. Make sure everything is tied down and that trip hazards have been eliminated.

Procedures

Have a start-up and shut-down procedure in your Boat Notebook in case someone besides yourselves must start up or shut down your engine and or generator. Any other procedures you can imagine a guest having to accomplish in an emergency should also be described and placed in your Boat Notebook.

Slip prevention

If your boat steps get slippery, consider applying non-skid. We have been very satisfied with Lewmar's nonskid mats on both our sailboat and on *L'Esprit*. We use it on steps as well as other slippery spots.

Lines and fenders

After you've left the dock, always make sure your lines are completely inside the boat and not hanging over the rails. Likewise, bring your fenders in so they don't drag in the water, knock against your hull, or, heaven forbid, cause other boaters to make fun of you.

Line storage

Learn to coil your lines and stow them in such a way they're easily accessed. Consider using chafe gear on your lines to prolong their life. Inside Passage waters experience significant winds at times, which cause extra wear and tear on your dock lines when tied to a marina. A good way to learn to neatly stow your lines is by going on YouTube and typing in "How to stow boat lines."

Cupboards

If you have any cupboards that have a tendency to open when underway, secure them in some fashion: better hardware, bungee cords, rubber gear ties, etc.

No-Fly Zone

Put away everything that can fly. Stow tea pots and other kitchen equipment in the galley sink. Make sure your floor is as clear as possible. This is especially important in sailboats, which routinely heel fifteen or more degrees when under way. This can create quite the mess down below if everything hasn't been stowed beforehand.

Electrical panel

Check the electrical panel from time to time. Know the pattern of what should be on during a passage, and what should be off. We, for example, rarely travel with our water pressure on. With the engines going, we'd never hear the pump chugging water into our bilge. Consider including a diagram in your Boat Notebook illustrating what should be on and off while at a marina, at anchor, and while underway.

Salvage rights

I urge you to know the salvage and towing laws of the countries in which you'll be cruising. In essence, if you need a tow, some unscrupulous salvors can make extreme monetary claims against you. I would suggest you talk with your boat insurer about the best ways to protect yourself against these sorts of claims if you ever need towing or salvaging. If you use a towing service such as SeaTow or BoatUS, discuss with them the best ways to protect yourself and your investment.

Keeping the Environment Healthy and Safe

Trash

In remote areas, you can burn on a beach during a rising tide. Watch for bears, wolves, burn bans, and other restrictions.

Moist, biodegradable trash can be minced and thrown overboard.

Store other trash in trash bags until you're in a marina that handles trash as part of its fee or for an additional charge. For example, at Refuge Cove you can motor over to Dave's Barge and pay him to take your bagged trash.

Remove as much packaging as you can when provisioning so you cut down on the amount of trash you have in the first place. When possible, separate your bottles and drink cans for recycling at marinas. Often collection of recyclable materials is free.

Politeness

Try to avoid ego battles, which really solve nothing and can actually create dangerous situations. Use your radio to communicate.

Radio protocol

There is no rule against you reading from a script when talking on a marine radio. At least until you get the hang of it, which in my case took more than a year. See chapter eleven and the Appendix for protocols and scripts. Your welcome!

Wakes

Wakes can create hazardous situations for other boats. You are responsible for your wake. If it causes damage, you may find yourself in court. Slow down for sailboats, kayakers, paddle boarders, etc.

Helping with lines

When in a marina, help incoming boats with their lines, especially if it is apparent no one else is. If someone is helping you with your lines, please give him instructions so they know what you want them to do. Try not to give your bow line to someone on the dock. If you must, ask them to keep it loose. Problems arise when a bow line is taken first and tightly tied to the dock; this forces the stern out, which can create real problems in a current. When helping with another boat's lines, listen for instructions and ask questions if needed. Make a single wrap around a cleat, rather than tying it off, while docking is still in process. Don't just hold a line and expect to be able to keep a boat steady. Winds and currents can make this difficult and dangerous. Treat others the way you want to be treated.

Helping others

If you see another boat in trouble, or about to have trouble, do what you can to help. Call them on the radio, hail them on your loud hailer, or honk to get their attention.

Dock safety

Try to keep your stuff off the docks. When in a marina, be courteous about what you put on the dock. Docks aren't necessarily wide, so if you take up a lot of space, others are deprived of the space they need. I remember coming into our dock once and I couldn't step onto the dock because our boat neighbors had piles of their stuff in the way. These people couldn't even help us land because there was little room for them to walk. It was scary for us, and they regretted making our landing difficult. Keep this in mind.

Offering advice

I suggest you curb your desire to offer advice, if you often have a strong urge to do so. Obviously there are times when advice must be given. But just because you think you have valuable advice, doesn't mean you do. On the other hand, your advice might be exactly what someone else needs. My advice: Ask people if they'd like your advice before giving it. (PS – I do get the irony of the last sentence!)

Sharing

If you see someone genuinely in need of water or food, or even entertainment, offer help if you can. One summer, during a drought when the island marinas were not making their water available, we made water for another boat that was running low. Again, treat people the way you want to be treated.

For Your Boat Notebook

- Boat Insurance information
- Towing and salvage services information
- Marine-radio scripts

Resources

- BoatUS.com/towing/Salvage
- SeaTow.com/marine-services/salvage
- BoatSafe.com
- AnimatedKnots.com

Chapter Eleven

Preparing to Cruise

Cruise Communications

Communicate with All Boats ★ Marine Radio Channels
Marine-Radio Channel Suggestions ★ Marine-Radio Scripts
Phones ★ Internet ★ Marine Weather

While cruising along the Inside Passage, you'll need communication devices to talk with other boats, ships, marinas, and the Coast Guard. You'll also want to be able to connect you're your family and friends at home, and make other social and business calls when needed. When you come into port, you'll want to contact the marina and other businesses in the area.

When we cruise, the communications issues that motivate me are being able to:

- Communicate with all boats, large or small, and with ship traffic, while on the water, and for them to be able to communicate with us.
- Communicate with land-based businesses and people while on the water.

- Use the Internet to receive and send information.
- Obtain the marine weather for the area I'm in.

Communicate with All Boats

Your boat should have at least one marine radio in order to talk to and hear from surrounding boats. Aboard *L'Esprit*, we have three: one fix-mounted and two handhelds. Some boats have more. The reasons for having more than one radio are:

- If one radio fails, you still have a radio (redundancy!)
- You'll be able to hear more than one channel at a time, which is helpful when you're making a passage through a lot of commercial traffic
- You'll want to take a handheld with you when travelling in your dinghy; if someone stays on the boat, that person will be able to receive your call.
- Sometimes you may need to make radio calls to other boats simultaneously.

Marine Radio Channels

In order to communicate with vessels, some marinas, and the Coast Guards of the US and Canada, you should have easy access to the marine radio channels for US and Canada. The primary channels you'll be using will be:

Washington VHF Channels

05A – Vessel Traffic Service Seattle – Northern Puget Sound
06 – Intership Safety

09 – Intership and Ship-shore all Vessels and Calling and Reply for Pleasure Vessels
13 – Vessel Bridge to Vessel Bridge – Large Vessels
14 – Vessel Traffic Service – So. Puget Sound
16 – International Distress, Safety, & Calling
22 – Coast Guard Liaison (to talk w/CG)
66A- Port Operations- (usually marinas)
67 – Intership for all vessels (US only)
68 – Intership and ship-shore, non-commercial
69 - Intership and ship-shore, non-commercial
72 – Intership only for all vessels (US only)
78 - Intership and ship-shore, non-commercial

British Columbia VHF Channels

05A – Vessel Traffic Service Seattle – Strait of Juan de Fuca west of Victoria
06-Intership Safety
09- Intership and ship-shore all vessels
11 – Vessel Traffic Service – North and east of Victoria
12- Vessel Traffic Service – Vancouver and Howe Sound
16- International Distress, Safety & Calling
66A- Port operations – usually marinas
67- Intership and ship-shore
68- Intership and ship-shore, non-commercial
69- Intership and ship-shore, non-commercial
71 – Vessel Traffic Service – Northern Strait of Georgia to Cape Caution
72 – Intership
73 – Intership and ship-shore
74 – Vessel Traffic Service Victoria – Victoria-Fraser River
83 – Coast Guard Liaison (talk w/CG)

For a complete list of all marine radio frequencies and their uses, go on Wikipedia and enter: Marine VHF Radio. When you scroll down, you'll find what you need. You can find a complete list of US frequencies if you Google "Navigation Center Maritime Telecommunications." Also, find these channels in this book's appendices.

Marine-Radio Channel Suggestions

If you're new to cruising, especially in the Pacific Northwest, you'll be glad to have some explanations regarding all these channels, as well as how and when to speak on a marine radio. Help is on the way! Here goes:

- No matter where you are in the PNW, if you want to talk to another boat or the Coast Guard, you'll use Channel 16. You won't be staying on Ch. 16, but that's always where you initiate it.
- Always keep your marine radio on Ch. 16. This way you can hear other boaters, ships, and the Coast Guard calling you. Plus, if you need to make a call, you'll need to be on Ch. 16 anyway.
- If you're cruising through areas where there's a lot of commercial traffic, you'll want to have your other radio on to Vessel Traffic Service (VTS) channel. You'll find a precise chart of where these VTS areas are near the front of your *Waggoner Cruising Guide*. You'll be monitoring these channels: Seattle Traffic, Ch.5A and 14; Vancouver Traffic, Ch.12; Victoria Traffic, Ch. 11; Comox Traffic, Ch.71; and Prince Rupert Traffic, Ch.71 and 11. Big ships move fast, but are also difficult to maneuver. Because of this, you can find yourself in

a pinch if you haven't been paying attention (i.e., listening to ship traffic). Tugs with barges look harmless until you realize you're on a collision course with one that can't just change its course because you're in the way. In other words, monitor the Vessel Traffic channel for the area you're in.
- When calling a marina on your marine radio, call the channel listed in your *Waggoner Cruising Guide*.
- When you want to talk with another boat, call them on Ch. 16. When they answer, they'll either suggest you switch to another channel, or they'll expect you to suggest another channel. If they suggest first, go to the channel they suggest. If they expect you to select a channel, choose either Ch. 9, 67, 68, 71, or 72
- If your boat is longer than 20 meters, the US Coast Guard requires that you monitor Ch. 13 (ship-to-ship) while in American waters. Even if your vessel's not that long you might want to guard Ch. 13 when you're in the vicinity of large ships.
- Do not have private conversations on Ch. 16. It is a hailing channel only.
- Do not make a radio check on Ch. 16. Instead use VHF Ch. 24, 25, 26, or 27
- Always be polite on the radio, even if you don't feel like it.
- Listen in before making a call so you don't step on someone else's call. Marine radios are two way radios.
- Practice using your installed marine radio's loud hailer and fog horn before departing the dock. You

don't want to be reading the user manual when you need to be calling out to another boat.

Marine-Radio Scripts

Communicating on a marine radio is totally different from talking on the telephone. In fact, when I first started boating decades ago, I refused to talk on the radio because I got stage fright. What got me over this terror was having a script to read from, which I'm going to share with now.

But before you read the scripts, here are some tips I've learned over the years:

- Talk in a normal tone. Yelling into the mike can make you more difficult to understand.
- Talk at a moderate pace. Speaking too fast and too slowly creates problems.
- The better you annunciate, the better you'll be understood.
- Have a pencil and paper handy near the radio.
- Have a device that displays your boat's GPS position near the radio.
- Say OVER to signal you've completed what you're going to say, but the conversation is not done.
- Say OUT to signal you're hanging up. (Don't say OVER AND OUT.)
- ROGER means yes.
- MAYDAY means real danger of loss of life or property.
- PON PON (pan pan) means nearing a real state of injury or loss of property.
- SECURITE SECURITE means there's a dangerous situation that boaters will want to know about.

- Marine radios often use NATO phonetic alphabet: Alpha, Bravo, Charlie, Delta, Foxtrot, Golf, Hotel, India, Juliet, Kilo, Lima, Mike, November, Oscar, Papa, Quebec, Romeo, Sierra, Tango, Uniform, Victor, Whiskey, X-ray, Yankee, Zulu.

Okay, as promised, here are your marine-radio scripts. We'll do a Mayday call first. Hopefully you'll never, ever need to make this call.

Mayday call:

MAYDAY MAYDAY MAYDAY This is power vessel My Boat, My Boat, My Boat. We are approximately one mile off the southern tip of Whidbey Island. Our engine caught on fire and we are taking on water. 40-foot Grand Banks, white hull, dark green canvas on top. Two people on board. Request immediate assistance. OVER.

Repeat in a minute or two if necessary.

In this, you have told the Coast Guard, in this order,

- Call type (Mayday)
- Vessel type and name (power, My Boat)
- Location (1 mile off Whidbey Island. Also you could give them your latitude and longitude)
- Vessel description (length, brand, color)
- Situation
- Number of people on board
- Your request

A couple of things to keep in mind:

- The Coast Guard may ask you to switch to another channel like 6 or 22a. Do so. In fact, practice

changing channels so in an emergency this is not hard.
- The Coast Guard may ask you questions regarding your position, life vests, health of those on board, number of people on board, etc.
- You may include others things besides what is written here. Do not do that until after you have established with the Coast Guard who and where you are.
- If your vessel's radio transmits your Automatic Identification System (AIS) information, you'll be more easily found. Also if you have an EPIRB, you might consider setting it off if you think you'll be difficult to find.

You should have this script in a prominent place in your Boat Notebook and somewhere near where you keep your marine radios. This way you can access the script, and so can your guests if they need to do so.

As suggested above, you should have a pre-printed Mayday script on your boat. Basically, here is what you need:

> MAYDAY MAYDAY MAYDAY This is SAIL/POWER vessel YOUR BOAT'S NAME. We are approximately LOCATION. We are SITUATION. We are a LENGTH, BRAND OR STYLE, COLOR. Request immediate assistance. OVER.

Pon Pon call

Use this when you are about to be in real danger, but you're not there yet.

PON PON, PON PON, PON PON. This is sailing vessel My Boat, My Boat, My Boat. One mile south of Whidbey Island. 40-foot Beneteau white with dark green trim. Two people onboard. Engine quit. Drifting to shore. Two people on board. Request immediate assistance. OVER

Repeat if you don't hear back in a couple of minutes.

In the above Pon Pon call, you have told the mariners in your vicinity, in this order:

- Call type (Pon Pon)
- Vessel type and name (sailing, My Boat)
- Location (1 mile off Whidbey Island. Also could give them your latitude and longitude)
- Vessel description (length, brand, color)
- Situation
- Number of people on board.
- Request

Securite call

Make a Securite call when you could be a danger to others, or they could be a danger to you, as in entering a tight channel where visibility is inhibited.

SECURITE SECURITE SECURITE This is 40-foot sailing vessel My Boat heading north through Dodd Narrows. All concerned traffic call My Boat on Ch. 16. OVER.

You do not have to repeat this call, and no one is required to answer you.

In the above Securite call, you have told boats in your vicinity:

- Call type (Securite)

- Vessel length, type, and name (40-foot sailing vessel My Boat)
- Location (heading north through Dodd Narrows.
- Request (concerned traffic call My Boat on Ch. 16)

Calling a marina

When calling a marina on your VHF radio, first check your *Waggoner* Cruising Guide for the frequency they use, if they use one at all; a lot of marinas use cell phones instead. Some marinas use both.

YOU: Friday Harbor Marina, Friday Harbor Marina, Friday Harbor Marina. This is the motor vessel My Boat, My Boat, My Boat. Over.

FH MARINA: My Boat, this is Friday Harbor Marina. OVER

YOU: Friday Harbor Marina, we are a 45-foot power boat looking for moorage tonight and tomorrow night. We would like a starboard tie and thirty amps of power. OVER.

FH MARINA: We have a spot for you. How far out are you? OVER

YOU: Approximately 2 miles. OVER

FH MARINA: Please call us when you are at the harbor entrance and we will give you your slip assignment. OVER .

YOU: Thank you, Friday Harbor Marina. We will call when we reach the harbor entrance. My Boat monitoring 66A. OUT.

FH MARINA: Friday Harbor monitoring 66A. OUT.

In the above call to a marina, you have:

- Hailed the marina and given them your boat's name.
- Heard the marina respond.
- Told the marina what you want (slip length; time span of request; the side you'd like to have tied to the dock, if any; and the amperage you'd like).
- Heard whether they can handle you or not.
- Told them where you are.
- Heard their request for when you can get your slip assignment.
- Thanked them, told them your intention to call, told them what channel you intend to monitor in case they want to get a hold of you, and affirmed you were closing the conversation by saying OUT.
- Heard the marina affirming the frequency they would be monitoring and that the conversation was ended by saying OUT.

Some additional notes about the above conversation that you'll want to know about are:

- You may have noticed that the normally 40-foot power vessel My Boat asked for a 45-foot slip. This is because it has a swim step off which the boat's line handler would step from the boat to the dock. My Boat realizes that a 40-foot slip would be too short, making it near impossible for the line handler to step onto the dock safely.
- Another reason My Boat asked for a longer slip than its actual size its dinghy hangs off its stern on davits, making My Boat several feet longer. Most

- marinas do not want your bow hanging over the dock where people heads could be bumped, or your stern hanging out in the fairway making it more difficult for other boats to maneuver.
- Be prepared with a pencil and paper when you call a marina. You'll want to write your slip assignment down along with any other information they give you.
- Be prepared with a diagram of the marina. Your navigation software should be very helpful, but you'll need to zoom way in. This underscores one of the reasons it's good to have at least two types of navigation software: one on your boat's main screen, and one on an iPad or tablet. The Burgee book dedicates itself to illustrating most marinas from Olympia to Port Hardy. *Waggoner Cruising Guide* has helpful diagrams for major marinas only. So does ActiveCaptain.com.
- Most marinas assume you to have some idea what their dock configuration is, but they also realize how distorted things can look from a boat. If you don't understand where they want you, ask them to give you landmarks or another explanation. They will be happy to oblige.

Calling a ship

If it looks like you and a ship or tug-and-barge are in danger of colliding, call the ship and ask its intention, and then tell it yours. If you know the name of the ship, use its name when calling. If you don't, call it by its location. Call the ship on Ch. 13 and/or 16. For example:

YOU: This is My Boat, My Boat, My Boat, calling the black-hulled freighter just off Turn Point, calling the black-hulled freighter just off Turn Point, calling the black-hulled freighter just off Turn Point. OVER.

SHIP: This is the freighter Endless Seas. OVER. (If you've called them on Ch. 16, they'll probably ask you to switch to Ch. 13.)

YOU: Endless Seas, we are the white powerboat approximately 2 nautical miles off your starboard bow. Our intention is to avoid you. What are your intentions? OVER

SHIP: Roger that. We plan to make a 20 degree turn to our port in 3 minutes. OVER

YOU: Copy that (or Roger that). Thank you, Captain, we will steer to our port to avoid you. OVER.

SHIP: Thank you. Endless Seas OUT.

YOU: My Boat back to 16. OUT.

In the above conversation with a ship, you have:

- Made known your boat's name and given a description of the ship you are calling because you don't know its name.
- Heard it respond to you.
- Explained who and where you are as well as your intentions. You have also explained to the ship what you need to know from it.
- Heard the ship's intentions.

- Confirmed that you heard the ship's intentions ("Copy that") and explained your intentions to the ship.
- Heard the ship end the conversation by saying OUT.
- Ended the conversation by saying OUT.

Some additional comments about the above boat-to-ship conversation that you'll want to know about are:

- There are several ways to learn a ship's name: 1) from its AIS blip on your navigation software, if it's capable of showing that;2) by calling Vessel Traffic Service (VTS) on Ch. 5A, 11, 12, 14, 71, or 74, depending on where you are; and 3) by setting one of your marine radios to the appropriate vessel traffic frequency for the area and listening in so you can hear ships tell vessel traffic where they are.
- Ships and tugs with barges are difficult to maneuver. If it looks like you have the right-of-way with one of these monsters, and it also looks that you're in danger of a colliding with one, forget your right-of-way advantage and get out of the way. Even better make it abundantly clear to them that you're planning to get out of the way by talking with them or by making an ultra-obvious course change.
- Ships are more than happy to have a conversation with you when you are nearby and there are appears to be some sort of danger. If they know you are aware of them, and you know they are aware of you, events tend to unfold more calmly.

- Every once in a while a ship will call you. For your safety, please answer them.
- Try to be up on marine-radio lingo (see below).

Marine-radio lingo

When calling large vessels, vessel traffic, as well as many fishing and recreational boats, you may hear marine radio lingo, as you read in the above conversation. "Copy that" and "Roger that" are examples of such lingo. Here's a list of phrases you'll commonly hear and will probably pick up yourself the more you cruise:

ROGER, ROGER THAT, COPY, COPY THAT – means you understand. It doesn't necessarily mean you agree or will comply, however.

WILCO –means you will comply. Don't use WILCO with either ROGER or COPY.

OVER – means you're done with your thought, but not the conversation.

OUT – means you're done with the whole conversation.

AFFIRMATIVE – means yes.

NEGATIVE – means no.

NINER – means nine and not to be confused with five.

SAY AGAIN, SAY AGAIN YOUR LAST – means please repeat.

STAND BY – means wait a minute

READY TO COPY – means ready to write something down.

BREAK – means you're starting a new thought.

Calling Vessel Traffic

Call Vessel Traffic when you want to know the name of a specific ship nearby and when you want a traffic update because you're crossing a heavily traversed passage. Also remember to call the Vessel Traffic frequency for the area you are in, either Ch. 5A, 11, 12, 14, 71, or 74. Your conversation with Vessel Traffic may sound something like this:

> YOU: Victoria Vessel Traffic, Victoria Vessel Traffic, Victoria Vessel Traffic. This is My Boat, My Boat, My Boat. OVER.
>
> VVT: My Boat, this is Victoria Vessel Traffic. OVER.
>
> YOU: Traffic, My Boat. We will be crossing northbound from Port Townsend to Cadboro Bay. We request a traffic update. OVER.
>
> VVT: Copy that, My Boat. The tanker Golden Ore is eastbound in Juan de Fuca Strait and the passenger vessel Alaska Pride is southbound nearing Beaumont Shoal. OVER
>
> YOU: Copy that, Traffic. Thank you. My Boat back to 16. OUT.
>
> VVT: Victoria Traffic OUT.

In the above conversation you have:

- Called Vessel Traffic on the appropriate channel and told them who you are.
- Heard Vessel Traffic acknowledge your call.
- Told Vessel Traffic where you are and what your request is. If you're requesting the name of a vessel instead of a traffic update, say "We are eastbound in Rosario Strait. What is the name of the ship heading north, near Deception Pass? OVER."

- Heard Vessel Traffic respond to your request.
- Acknowledged receiving the information, expressed thanks, informed Vessel Traffic of the channel you will be monitoring, and signaled that the conversation is over.
- Heard Vessel Traffic acknowledge that the conversation is over.

Some additional comments about the above boat-to-Vessel Traffic conversation that you'll want to know about are:

- When talking the Vessel Traffic, be sure to have your charts out. Vessel Traffic will describe ship locations by latitude and longitude and by proximity to buoys and landmarks.
- Ships and tugs must report to Vessel Traffic between fifteen and forty-five minutes before navigating a Vessel Traffic Service Area. They have to give the vessel's name, type, position, destination, intended route, and estimated time of arrival.
- Before calling Vessel Traffic, listen to it for a couple of minutes to get a lay of the land, I mean sea.

Calling the Coast Guard

When calling the Coast Guard, always call on Ch. 16, whether in Canada or the United States. Besides experiencing an emergency, you might call the Coast Guard to report dangers you spot in the water, such as deadheads, large debris, boat parts, etc. Your conversation with the Coast Guard will sound something like this:

YOU: Canadian Coast Guard, Canadian Coast Guard, Canadian Coast Guard. This is My Boat, My Boat, My Boat. OVER.

CCG: My Boat, this is the Canadian Coast Guard. Are you in any danger? OVER

YOU: No (or negative). OVER

CCG: Switch to 83. OVER.

YOU: Switching to 83. OVER. (at the point, switch to 83, and call the Coast Guard again).

YOU: Canadian Coast Guard, this is My Boat on Channel 83. OVER.

CCG: This is Canadian Coast Guard. OVER.

YOU: Canadian Coast Guard, I'd like to report a large deadhead floating outside the entry to Pender Harbour. OVER.

CCG: Copy. What is its approximate latitude and longitude? OVER

YOU: (speaking slowly) 49 04 31 north, 12 21 55 west. OVER

CCG: Copy. We will broadcast that for mariners in the vicinity. OVER.

YOU: Copy. My Boat back to 16. OUT.

CCG: Canadian Coast Guard monitoring 16. OUT.

In the above conversation you:

- Called the Coast Guard and told them who you are.
- Heard them acknowledge your call and ask if you are in immediate danger.

- Told them you are not in danger.
- Heard them ask you to switch channels so your conversation does not happen on the emergency channel.
- You acknowledged the new channel number and switched your radio to that channel.
- You recalled the Coast Guard and repeated who you are.
- Heard them acknowledge receiving your call.
- Told them of a navigation hazard you spotted as you entered Pender Harbour.
- Heard the Coast Guard ask you for a more specific location for the hazard.
- Gave the hazard's approximate latitude and longitude according to your navigation software or GPS.
- Heard the Coast Guard acknowledge receiving the latitude and longitude and telling you'll they will transmit the information to local mariners.
- Acknowledged what they said, reported that you were going back to Ch. 16, and signaled the conversation was over by saying OUT.
- Heard the Coast Guard signal it was returning to monitor Ch. 16 and the conversation was over by saying OUT.

Some additional comments about the above boat-to-Coast Guard conversation that you'll want to know about are:

- The Coast Guard will probably want more information from you than what is indicated in the above conversation. Be ready with your vessel's ID

number and other personal information. The Coast Guard understandably wants to insure the legitimacy of you and your report.
- There may be times when you report an emergency which does not put you in immediate danger, but clearly someone else is in peril. For example you see another boat has caught on fire, a whale has overturned another boat, or you find someone floating at sea. In case such a situation arises, when you call the Coast Guard let them know the situation early in the conversation. Also, be as helpful as you can after the call. Do unto others . . . .

Calling another vessel

Most of your calls will be to other recreational vessels. If you're cruising with friends, it's only natural that you'll call each other several times during passages. You might also call boats which you think might be on a collision course, or boats whom you perceive to have a problem they are unaware of, or boats you just want to ask a question about. In all instances, the conversation starts and ends like this:

YOU: Seabolt, Seabolt, Seabolt. This is My Boat, My Boat, My Boat. OVER

THEM: Seabolt here. OVER.

YOU: Switch to 72. OVER

THEM: Copy. Switching to 72. OVER. (You both switch to 72)

YOU (or them): Seabolt. This is My Boat. OVER.

THEM: Hey, how the heck are you? OVER

YOU: Great! (Your conversation can be very natural now, because you are no longer on the emergency or ship channels.) OVER

YOU at end of conversation: My Boat back to 16. OUT.

THEM: Seabolt back to 16. OUT

In the above conversation you:

- Stated the name of the boat you were hailing and you stated your name.
- Heard the boat you hailed acknowledge your call.
- Asked the other boat to switch to a dedicated boat chat channel (i.e., Ch. 72).
- Heard them acknowledge the new channel.
- Both switched to the new channel
- Hailed each other back and had your conversation.
- Indicated the conversation was over and that you were going back to Ch. 16.
- Heard the other boat indicate the conversation was over and was going back to Ch. 16.

Some additional comments about the above boat-to-boat conversation that you'll want to know about are:

- There are a lot of possible channels on which you can have boat-to-boat conversations: 9, 68, 69, 71, 72, 78, 79, 80.
- If, when you are signing off on a conversation, your boat is monitoring more than one radio channel because you have more than one radio on, you may say, "My Boat, monitoring Ch. 16 and 13," or "My Boat returning to Ch. 16 and 13."

- There is no rule you can't listen in on the conversations of strangers. It's definitely not polite. Regardless, know that when you talk on the marine radio, others can listen to your conversations, even when it is on a boat-to-boat channel.
- If you are cruising with several other boats, you can all be in on a conversation by listening to where the radios are routed (Ch. 9, 68, 69, 71, 72, 78, 79, 80). You just have to be patient so as not to step on or talk over each other. Only one person can talk at a time on a marine radio.
- If you have children on board, keep the marine radio away from them! Channel 16 is an emergency channel. If they are playing with the radio and it is on Ch. 16, people in real emergencies cannot get the help they need. The Coast Guard can trace you. They get very upset if they have to trace you because your children are on the radio.

Communicate with Land-Based Businesses and People While on the Water

Besides your marine radio, you'll need to use your cell phone while cruising. Many marinas ask that you call them on the phone rather than the marina radio. There are times when you'll need to call your bank, your family, your boat-repair person, or the manufacturer of a device you have on the boat.

If you're cruising within your own country and you're remaining somewhat close to civilization, your present cell phone should work fine. Just make sure your plan provides you plenty of data coverage as well.

But if you're cruising outside your country and venturing into the wild, and if being able to make and receive phone calls is important to you, here are a few suggestions:

- Because technology changes constantly, what you're reading this very moment may have already changed. With that in mind, consider calling your present carrier and ask them about using their services in the country you'll be visiting.
- Because the population density in area north of Nanaimo and Pender Harbour becomes more and more sparse, there will be fewer and fewer cell phone towers. For example, the cruising area north of Port Hardy and south of Prince Rupert, which is about five-hundred miles, there are, at the time of this writing, four cell phone towers: Bella Bella, Hartley Bay, Oona, and Bella Coola. Clearly, as you venture north of Nanaimo and into SE Alaska, cell phone reception is often poor or unavailable. For a visual of coverage along the Inside Passage, visit OpenSignal.com.
- If you really need a phone, consider purchasing a satellite phone. We have two of them because, for various reasons, we need to have a phone in the wild. The reason we have two is because their satellites are configured quite differently, so when one doesn't work, the other one does. It's expensive, but it's what we need to do in order to

make and receive phone calls in the wild. The two we use are Iridium and GlobalStar. It is possible to send and receive text messages on satellite phones.
- Just as we have two satellite services, we also purchased an AT&T GoPhone, which we prepay when we travel in Canada and Alaska. That way when our Verizon phone isn't picking up reception, the AT&T GoPhone will. Verizon also offers the Verizon PrePaid, which like the GoPhone has no annual contract. We just call up AT&T and pay for the service we want for the length of time we want it. If you're cruising outside your own country, I'd suggest you consider purchasing a prepaid cell phone service from a carrier with good coverage in the country you're visiting.
- I'd also suggest you consider installing a cell-phone booster. Not only does it boost your calls, it also boosts your data connectivity. We have a Wilson and are happy with it, but there are others. Whichever you purchase, make certain you buy marine grade so it won't deteriorate in the salt-water environment.

Use the Internet to Receive and Send Information

When out cruising, it really can feel as though you're cut off from the rest of the world, because, well, you are. The one thing that can bring the world back into your life is the Internet. You'll want it to be able to receive it on your Smartphone, your tablet, and your computer.

As a cruiser, you'll especially want Wi-Fi to access:
- Email.
- World and local news.
- Weather – Weather4D.com, PassageWeather.com, ForecastWeather.gov, PredictWind, OceanWeather.com, NWS.noaa.gov.
- Complete business transactions, such as banking, bill paying, etc.
- Update your blog and/or social media (i.e., Facebook, Instagram, etc.).
- Download apps to your Smartphone, tablet, or computer.

While we're on the subject of apps, let me suggest a few that you might want to preload on your devices. Some are free, while some are not. Some require you to have Internet access or data roaming or a device with an internal GPS, while others don't. I am simply going to list apps that I consider worthy without much explanation. I assume that by the time this book goes to print, at least half of these apps will have changed for the better in terms of accessibility and range of use, and new ones will have come on the market. Regardless, here goes:

Navigating programs and apps:

PocketNav, Charts and Tides, Active Captain Cruising Guidebook, Navionics, iSailor, Nobeltec's TimeZero, MXMariner, Rose Point's, CoastalNavigator, Memory-Map, GPSLongDistanceLog, CourseToSteer, Garmin's BlueChart, NavX, SEAiq.

Anchor watch:

MyAnchorWatch, DragQueenAnchorAlarm, MagneticBearing, Anchor Alert.

AIS:

SmartChartAIS, BoatWatch, MarineTraffic, BoatBeacon.

Laptop chart plotting:

Navigatrix.

Weather:

MarineWeather, WindNOAA, PredictWind, PocketGrib, WeatherTrack.

Tides and currents:

AyeTides.

Reference:

CruisersForum, BoatersPocketReference, NavigationLightsAndShapes, NauticalChartSymbols

Sailing:

PointsOfSail, SailSim, HistoryOfSailing, SailingFlashcards.

Emergency:

BoatUS, SOSMorseCodeFlashlight, GPSTrackingPro.

Celestial navigation:

Celestial, StarWalk.

Note: Two great one-stop places to research the above information are BoatUS.com and ActiveCaptain.com. Explore their sites! And equally good, even though they do have a commercial bias, is Westmarine.com.

I'm also going to suggest that while you are in the marinas north of Nanaimo and Pender Harbour, that you not download movies and television programs. These marinas have limited bandwidth. When you download a movie or television program via the Internet, you are robbing your fellow boaters of Internet access. Please consider downloading movies and television programs before your depart on your cruise, and then read the latest news rather than watching it.

None of the above are be possible if you can't access the Wi-Fi or data. There are several solutions for this:

- A marine-grade Wi-Fi booster, like Wi-Fi Rogue Wave and The Wirie AP+, is one possibility.
- Use your smart phone as a Wi-Fi hotspot, while using a cell phone booster (Wilson) to increase reception. We ended up doing this after spending a lot of money on the Rogue Wave Wi-Fi booster. Still, keep in mind that technology improves rapidly nowadays.
- Even better, use a pocket Wi-Fi hotspot from your cell phone provider or purchase or rent a SkyRoam or similar product. These hotspots don't chew up your phone's battery life, which is important. They're great when they work, but be prepared for them not working when you're out in middle of whale and bear country. Plus, when you do your other travelling, these little hotspots give you secure Wi-Fi access for at least five devices. Again, technology is constantly working to improve these products' range and versatility.

One benefit all three of the above provide password-secure Wi-Fi, which is important when you're completing business transactions with your bank or credit card company, or any time you don't want neighboring boats or townspeople to access your device.

Hearing Marine Weather for the Area

One of the most important things you'll be accessing is reliable weather data on your marine radio, smart phone, iPad/tablet, and laptop. Here are some ideas I hope you'll find useful:

Have a spiral binder or writing book dedicated to collecting weather data you hear on the marine radio.

Listen to the marine weather report several times a day, and record what you hear each time. (More on this in the weather chapter.)

To hear weather on your radio, press the radio's WX button, and then change channels until you can hear the recording. Usually your radio picks up the report closest to it, which is probably, but not always, the one you want to listen to.

Refer to your *Waggoner Cruising Guide* for weather radio broadcast channels and phone numbers; these change from one area to the next.

When your mobile data are functioning, click into the Internet, and then click into either Canadian Weather or NOAA, depending where you are. You should have both of these sites Bookmarked in your device before you leave home. When you click into either country's weather, select the report you want, then save the page as a PDF, or do a screen save. That way you can read it at your leisure.

When your iPad or tablet can access a weather predicting app, also do a screen-save, or rather, do several of them. One for today, one for tomorrow, one for the next day, and so on. Sure, the actual weather forecast will probably change as time progresses, but you'll have at least something to go by.

For Your Boat Notebook

- Marine-radio channels to use
- Marine-radio scripts

Resources

- Waggoner *Cruising Guide*
- BoatUS.com
- ActiveCaptain.com
- Westmarine.com

Chapter Twelve

Preparing to Cruise

Insurance

Boat Insurance ★ Home and Car Insurance
Health Insurance.

Granted, insurance is a pain in the neck, but if you don't make sure your current policies aren't up to date, or if you don't have sufficient coverage, there's a fifty-fifty chance that you'll wish you had. This means the policies that cover your home and boat, as well as your life, your health, and even your car.

The primary possible events that motivate me regarding insurance are:

- Having a boating incident in which we discover too late that we are not covered
- Having the tools to receive the help we need in case or a health issue

- Feeling confident that my home and car are safe while we're gone

Boat Insurance

You'll want to make sure your boat insurance covers:

- The full-replacement cost of your boat.
- The costs included in case your boat experiences a mechanical breakdown while cruising.
- The peripheral costs in case of an accident, such as pollution and wreckage removal.
- The places you are going when you are going. Tell your agent your plans. For example, on our recent trip to Alaska, we couldn't go north of Port McNeil until after April 20, 2016. If we'd gone further before that time and had an accident, we wouldn't have been covered.

You'll also want to make sure you have on board and do the things your insurance policy requires of you to maintain your coverage:

- Your safety equipment is all up-to-date.
- Your navigation products are on board, including charts.
- You travel when it's safe, and stay put when it's predicted not to be (i.e., don't venture out into storms).

Home and Car Insurance

You'll want to make sure these policies:

- Are up-to-date and paid up for the duration of your cruise.

- You'll also want to have someone who'll routinely check on your house and mail while you're gone. This person should have your phone and boat information, and have instructions on how to contact the US or Canadian Coast Guard if necessary to locate you.
- In addition, you might want to check with your car insurance if you're going on a trip that lasts over a month. You may get a break on your insurance while you're gone. The same goes for cable television, if you have it. Check with your carrier to see if you can stop your service while you're gone.

Health Insurance

With regard to your health insurance while cruising, it's a good idea to:

- Let your health insurance know to where you're cruising and how long you'll be gone.
- Make sure you're covered in case you need a medical evacuation while in the wilds. Consider adding coverage such as The Air Rescue Card, LifeMed Alaska, SkyMed, InsureMyTrip.
- Make copies of all medical insurance cards and put in your Boat Notebook.
- Take into consideration that US health insurance cannot be used in Canada, and vice versa. Medicare definitely does not work. Ask your health insurance provider about international coverage, or seek it from an outside provider.

Also regarding your health, visit your doctor before you leave on your cruise. At this visit:

- Make sure you have an adequate amount of your usual prescription drugs.
- Ask your doctor for the following prescriptions: pain reducer, muscle relaxant, general antibiotic for use until medical services can be found when out in the wild.

For Your Boat Notebook

- Copies of medical insurance cards
- List of all prescriptions you have on board, and their purpose.
- List of phones numbers for the people you'd need to contact in case of a medical emergency or accident.

Chapter Thirteen

Preparing to Cruise

Finances and Mail

Paying Bills on Time ★ Credit Card Safety
Beneficial Credit Cards ★ Snail Mail
Getting Cash ★ Boat Cards

If your cruise takes you away from home for a couple of weeks, getting your finances in order is a lot simpler than if you're planning to be gone three or four months. Being gone for a month or longer means that unexpected bills and mail can appear for which you may incur a penalty for not attending to it.

When we on *L'Esprit* plan to be gone for more than a month, we try to think of everything that can go wrong, big or small, and deal with it ahead of time.

In other words, these are our primary motivators when considering our finances:

- All bills get paid on time, thus not incurring penalties and interest.
- Our credit cards are safe

- Our credit cards will work for us throughout our travels, including exchange rates when we travel to a foreign country.
- All our mail is saved, and mail we need to know about comes to our attention quickly.
- We have the cash we need.

Paying Bills on Time

Because your banking needs aren't necessarily the same as my banking needs, I would suggest that you contact your bank(s), credit union(s), and credit card company(s) a couple of months before you head out. At least ask them about:

- Their online banking program and how it functions.
- The possibility of adjusting your credit limits for the period you're cruising.
- Their foreign transaction fees, which are often higher than credit unions.
- How to safely make transfers while in a foreign port.
- How to safely get account data while cruising.
- What other banks they affiliate with is the area you'll be visiting.

After you gather the above information, make a list of all the ways you'll be responsible for a payment:

- Recurring bills (i.e., rent or mortgage, car payment, home utilities)
- Expected bills for purchases you make up until your date of departure

- Cruising bills which you incur while cruising

Then decide how you'll satisfy each of the above.

Recurring bills

Prepay either with pre-dated written checks or online banking. You may consider having a trusted family member, friend, or mail service post these payments for you.

Expected bills

Over pay these bills days before you depart. You decide how much leeway you want to give yourself in case you've forgotten a purchase you made.

Cruising bills

While cruising, keep all receipts. When away, either access the amount you owe via Internet or phone and mail in bill, or overpay your credit card and use the excess to pay for your trip. (If you are in a foreign country, make certain you have stamps for that country, which can be difficult to obtain if you're in a remote area. Purchase foreign stamps at your first opportunity.)

Another method to ensure your ongoing bills get paid is by opening a bank account in the country you're visiting. We have never done this, but have cruising friends that have and swear by the practice. So I pass it on to you.

Credit-Card Safety

After having cruised in the Inside Passage for the last half decade, I have learned a couple of important things about cruising with credit cards.

First, call all your credit card companies and tell them when you're expected to be cruising. Do this so they don't automatically shut down your card when they see a strange purchase made in a place they don't expect you to be. You can't blame them for doing that, but it's very annoying when they call you before shutting off your card and you're out in the middle of Georgia Strait or climbing you mast to straighten a halyard.

Second, we have at least one credit card whose company we ask to not cut off our card unless we call and make the request. We've learned to do this because we have had credit cards cut off for the simple reason that we couldn't answer the credit company's phone call because we had no reception. Which also meant couldn't call the credit card company because our cell phone wouldn't work. This is not necessarily a problem experienced in an urban area. Out in the wild west of the Inside Passage, it's common. Take the precaution and request one credit card company not cut you off.

Third, we limit the cards we use. We usually take three cards with us, but only use one consistently. Because we use it for fuel, groceries, restaurants, and marina fees, and because I write down all purchases we make in my own cruise log, we know what the trip is costing us. And we know where the credit card is at all times.

Fourth, if you want to access your banking online in a marina, be careful. You may want to use your phone as a Wi-Fi hotspot, thus giving you more security. Or you may want to use a portable Wi-Fi roamer like SkyRoam, which frankly doesn't work as often as your phone in the wilds of the Inside Passage (but they're trying to improve that).

Some Credit Cards are More Beneficial than Others

When you make purchases in your own country, your credit card company doesn't charge you an exchange fee. But when you travel in a foreign country, it does.

Because we have found that not all credit card company's charge the same exchange fee, it would behoove you to find out which of your cards charges the least. In our case, the USAA and the Schools First cards charge the least. So they're the first ones we turn to when traveling in a foreign country.

Snail Mail is Still Important

There're a few ways you can handle mail while you're gone for an extended period, and they're fairly straight forward.

First, if you'll only be gone for a few weeks, and you're not worried about getting time-sensitive mail, you can have the post office collect it. If you're Canadian, Google Canada Post Hold Mail, and you'll be led to the page where you can sign up while still in your pajamas and sipping a cup of coffee. If you're American, you can sign up on line by Googling USPS Hold Mail. There's usually a time limit on how long your local post office will hold your mail, so make certain of your itinerary before you sign up.

Second, you can hire someone to collect your mail and sort through it. We do this. Martha comes to our home a couple of times a week, brings in the mail, and makes sure things look as they should. She has all our itinerary information in case she needs to contact us about any mail that looks suspect in terms of time-sensitivity.

Third, you can hire a mail-forwarding service in your area. We have friends who do this, and are quite satisfied. There's a private mail-box service in town which will forward mail at designated times to designated places. It's not free, of course. You'd have to rent one of their mail-boxes, you'd have to have a itinerary you're willing to adhere to, and you'd have to supply them with legitimate places to where your mail can be shipped and saved for you. That's a lot of pre-arranging, but if it's what you need to keep your life running smoothly, it's a great solution.

If you plan to have your mail forwarded, I'd suggest that you talk with the targeted post office, FedEx, UPS, or DHL so you know if they have any special requirements for receiving and holding your package.

Getting Cash

The first year we cruised into Canada from the US, I went to the bank a month before departure and ordered $1500 in Canadian cash, which is extremely beautiful, by the way. It's a good thing I went early because it took several weeks for the cash to arrive. And the bank charged me a lot for this service, in my opinion.

The next year, I didn't get more cash because we still had at least half of the original amount.

But the third year, we asked our credit card and credit union companies where we could get cash in Canada. When we discovered these locations, our life became much easier.

However, if you're travelling north of Pender Harbour, Campbell River, and Port McNeil, please know your opportunities to meet an ATM face-to-face diminish greatly until you find yourself in Prince Rupert and Ketchikan.

One More Thing – Boat Cards

Consider making yourselves some boat cards. You'll be meeting a lot of people on your cruise, and you'll probably want to swap information with them. Having a boat card makes this easy.

You'll, of course, want to consider what you want printed on your card. Some people include their home address, while some don't. Most cruisers do include their:

- Names.
- Cell-phone numbers.
- E-mail addresses.
- Boat's name along with its picture.
- You decide what you want.

You can have them printed by Vista Print or another online company. Or you can print them out yourself using your computer and printer.

Give your boat card to the people at home who may need to get hold of you. It might come in handy for them.

For Your Boat Notebook

- List of places to mail and receive mail
- List of ATM and bank locations which you might need

Chapter Fourteen

Preparing to Cruise

Your Boat's Fluids

Fuel System ★ Engine and Generator Systems
Fresh-Water System ★ Septic System
Galley ★ Batteries
Steering System ★ Dinghy
Anchor System ★ Sailing Systems

Your boat has so many different vital fluids I'm going to be listing them here for you. And because they're vital, you'll want to not only check them frequently, you'll want keep an on-going list in your Boat Notebook (or Captain's log) of each fluid's customary levels and brand, and when additions and changes are made. Whoever's responsibility the engine is, should probably be the keeper of this information. On *L'Esprit*, this information is kept in the Captain's Log. I keep a copy in the Boat Notebook.

As First Mate, my prime motivators when it comes to boat fluids are:

- Knowing what each fluid's optimum and dangerously-low levels are.
- Knowing exactly what each fluid's type and/or brand is.
- Knowing where each fluid is stored on the boat, and where it can be purchased.
- Knowing when each fluid is changed or added to, and by how much.
- Knowing when leaks have occurred and when they were repaired.

Whether you're cruising on a sailboat or a powerboat, your chariot has lots of systems that require fluids to operate properly. Here are the areas you as First Mate and the Captain will want to keep track of and maintain:

The Fuel System

Know your fuel system's maximum capacity; the type of fuel (diesel or gasoline); the preferred additive brand(s) and ratio per gallon/liter. Top off your fuel before leaving on long cruise. Also, top off at the end of the season to lessen chance of condensation developing in fuel tank during cold winter weather.

The Engine and Generator Systems

Know the appropriate oil, coolant, and transmission oil brands and levels and when additions are made and should be made. Top off these fluids before leaving on long cruise. Also note any discrepancies that occur from one year to the next.

Fresh-Water System

Know your tank's capacity, and top off before leaving. Add a teaspoon or so of bleach to keep the water bacteria free. If you have a water maker, note the manufacturer's suggested lubricants, if any.

Septic System

Your septic system may run on fresh water from your water maker or water tank, or it uses sea water.

If your head uses sea water, you'll want to add vinegar (not bleach) to help prevent scale, which can eventually block the hose to the holding tank. To prevent grasses and sea life from entering your boat, along with the sea water, consider putting a strainer at the intake.

In any case, read your head's user manual and take its recommendations seriously. Most heads need lubrication, and you'll do yourself a favor by having a lubricant that's right for your head. Avoid using mineral oil, because it's a petroleum product that will harm parts of your head.

As stated in an earlier chapter, we use Zaal's NoFlex Digestor Sewage Treatment in your holding tank. It does what its name says: it digests your raw sewage and renders it transparent, but not drinkable. For information, Google Zaal Noflex.

Galley

If your galley is non-electric, make sure you have enough propane and natural gas for stove, oven, and grill.

Batteries

Check to make sure that your batteries' water levels are full; keep track of when you add distilled water, and note discrepancies from previous years.

Steering system

If applicable, add steering fluid and lubricant.

Dinghy

Make sure you have adequate fuel for your dinghy engine stored in red portable fuel tanks. If you're using an additive, know the ratio per gallon to use, and know where the additive is stored, and its specific brand and information.

Anchoring System

Have on hand the correct gear grease or machine oil (read manufacturer's instructions) for lubricating your wench's gears. Also have the correct oil for your anchor swivel, if you have one. We have a Suncor Stainless Steel 360 Degree Anchor Swivel; on long cruises Capt. Dave oils it frequently to receive its optimum effect.

Sailing Systems

Check and add lubricants, greases, and oils for wenches and sail tracks.

For Your Boat Notebook

- List of fluids and other products your boat requires, along with their specific brand and information, and where on the boat each is stored.
- History of fluids changes and replacement information.

Chapter Fifteen

Preparing to Cruise

Tool Kits

Cabin Maintenance ★ Boat-Systems Maintenance
Miscellaneous

Obviously how you organize your tools depends on your boat and your work style. Some boaters organize by type of tool, while others sort their tools by where and when each is usually needed. You may find that you begin to organize your tools one way, but change when you discover another way is more suitable to you.

My primary motivators, when it comes to tools, are:

- Having what we'll need when we're out in the middle of nowhere
- Knowing where each tool is
- Knowing how and when to use each tool

Because your boat is both your home and your means of transportation, the tools you'll need on board range from hole-punches and little screw drivers to repair glasses, to heavy maul hammers and gigantic wrenches.

So that you're not overwhelmed by the following list, I'm going to divide it up by use. There will be some overlap, but you'll get the point.

Maintaining the House

- Small screw-driver set with a couple sizes of Phillips and slotted screw drivers. I use one that has fold-out drivers so it's hard to lose parts. It comes in handy for tightening cupboard handles, among other things.
- Small long-nose pliers.
- Metal clippers.
- Fabric scissors that are labeled so they're not use for cutting paper.
- Paper scissors.
- Utility scissors.
- **Pencil box** large enough to hold a small hole punch, small stapler, pencil sharpener, glue gun and glue, white glue, scotch tape, hole reinforcements, X-Acto or craft knife, paper clips, postage stamps for the country in which you'll be cruising, and envelops (you may need to store these elsewhere).
- **Floor cleaning tools**: broom, mop, vacuum, small whisk broom and dust pan.
- **Toilet cleaning tools**: toilet brush and caddy, micro rags, cleaning fluid compatible with your boat's hose materials, holding tank treatments such as NoFlex.
- **Window-cleaning** tools: squeegee, microfiber cloths, window cleaner.

- **Dish-cleaning tools**: pot scrubber, micro cloths, sponges, detergents, Steel Glo for stove and sink, dryer sheets to help soaking pans clean up even faster and better, mesh drain strainer, dish drying pad and/or rack, quick-drying towels. Perhaps a collapsible wash basin and collapsible drainer.
- **Trash-handling tools**: plastic bags, trash bins, counter-top composter (see chapter ten).
- **Food storage**: re-sealable plastic bags in various sizes, non-re-sealable plastic bags and clips (I love Ikea's Bevara clips), plastic containers with lids, tin foil, and plastic wrap (I swear by Stretch Tite). When you really need food to last, have on board a mini-computer vacuum and/or a vacuum sealer to suck out air from bags.
- **Cooking tools**. (See Ch. 9)
- **Laundry tools**: detergent, stain remover, (a paste of Dawn detergent and hydrogen peroxide often works miracles – thank you, Kim!) softener, clothes hangers, clothes line, laundry bag, clothes pins, and a sewing kit. If you have a washer and dryer on board, have on board items they require for optimum use.
- **Surface cleaning tools**: micro dust rags, duster, all-purpose cleaner in spray bottle or not (according to your preference), cleaning brushes, stain remover like Folex.
- **Electrical and electronic tools**: extra light bulbs; batteries; 12 volt and AC rechargers as needed for phones, computers, tablets, radios.

- **Manuals** for all appliances (may be printed from Internet and kept in notebook for easy access).
- **Plumbing tools:** Rescue Tape; your toilet brand's service kit; wrenches, screw drivers, pliers, hose clamps from engine tools; plumbers grease from engine tools; extra valves.
- **General lubricants and fluids:** WD 40, 3-in-1 oil, vinegar, distilled water, Simple Green (degreaser), and bleach.

Maintaining the Boat's Systems

For most repairs you'll probably need:

- Complete (metric and SAE) sets of crescent, open-end, and Allen wrenches
- Complete socket set and driver set
- Crimping, needle nose, and vise-grip pliers in various sizes
- Wire cutters
- Hammers
- Saws
- Files
- Channel locks in various sizes
- WD 40
- Soldering iron, solder, and maybe flux
- Pipe compound
- Headlamp, flashlights, and trouble light
- Duct, rigging, electrical, Teflon, and rescue tape
- Contact cleaner for batteries
- Bulbs for running and anchor lights
- Engine oil
- Coolants

- Pencil zincs
- Spare water pump and alternator.

For more specific problems, you may find you need:

- **Sail repair**: sail repair tape, straight and curved needles, Dacron thread, sewing palm, and scissors.
- **Electrical repairs**: digital multimeter, the appropriate marine-grade wire, electric tape, crimp terminals, spare fuses and breakers, wire stripper, and wire crimper.
- **Prop repairs**: face mask, hack saw, ball-peen hammer, puller, and adjustable wrench (hope you never need to do this!).
- **Stuffing-box repair**: appropriate wrenches.
- **Windlass repair**: brass wire brush, 400-grit wet/dry sandpaper, spray-on corrosion inhibitor or dielectric grease, joint compound, replacement lugs, and chain hook.
- **Overheating:** channel lock or needle-nosed pliers, impeller puller, spare impellers, spare raw water pump and/or replacement seals and bearings, replacement belts, assortment of hose clamps, snap ring pliers, hex wrenches, V-belt, IR temperature sensor
- **Fuel-filter repair**: filter wrench, spare filter parts, open-ended wrenches, strap wrench (if spin-on primary filter), bowl wrench (if manufacturer produces one), appropriate drive sockets and wrenches, extra filter elements, and extra primary and secondary filters.

- **Outboard repair**: pliers, extra spark plugs, plug wrench, shear pin.
- **Manuals** for all engines and major products (may be printed from Internet and kept in notebook for easy access).
- **Plumbing repair**: Teflon tape or thread sealant, spare hoses, hose clamps, Rescue tape, appropriate wrenches, and spare pumps.
- **Dinghy repair**: dinghy repair kit, spare starter cord, and spare drain plug.
- **Rigging repair**: spare rivets, wire cutters, silicone, spreader, and rigging tape, bosun's chair, pulley system for hauling up bosun's chair, cable cutters, crimp tool, and tension gauge.
- **Sail repair**: sail repair tape and sail repair kit (sailor's palm, needles, twine, and thread).
- **Lighting**: Have extra bulbs handy. Consider purchasing LED bulbs because they are great energy savers for lighting your navigation lights, as well as your interior lights. They cost more than regular bulbs, but they use so little electricity, they're worth it. Especially for you anchor light, which can eat up a lot of electricity because it's on all night.

Miscellaneous Tools

- Ironwood Pacific's Top-Snapper Tool for snapping hard-to-snap canvas only your boat.
- Hatchet.
- Scissors and shears.

- Retrieval tools for when things that have fallen into the bilge.
- Moisture Meter.
- Loctite Thread Locker.
- Bolt cutters for sailboat rigging.

For Your Boat Notebook

- List of all tools on board and where they are stored
- Manuals (you may want to place these in a separate notebook, or two – on *L'Esprit* our manuals take up four notebooks)
- Printouts from Internet (i.e., from WestMarine.com) of how to make specific repairs
- List of Need-To-Acquire tools

Resources

- The publications for discovering and repairing boat issues
- Nigel Calder's *Boatowner's Mechanical and Electrical Manual: How to Maintain, Repair, and Improve Your Boat's Essential Systems*
- Don Casey's *Complete Illustrated Sailboat Maintenance Manual: Including Inspecting the Aging Sailboat, Sailboat Hull and Deck Repair*
- Internet links to: CruisersWiki.org > Wiki Contents > Yacht Maintenance, WestMarine.com
- All manuals for your boat's systems and products.

Chapter Sixteen

Preparing to Cruise

Managing Customs

Paperwork in Order ★ Estimate Arrival Time
Declaring Items ★ Document Everything
Visible Proof ★ Courtesy Flags

Whether you're going from the United States into Canada, or vice versa, you'll have a much easier experience if you are prepared ahead of time.

As *L'Esprit*'s First Mate, my primary motivations when passing through customs are to:

- Be organized, and therefore calm.
- Be helpful to the customs agent.
- Be honest and respectful of each country's rules and regulations.
- To be law-abiding and welcome in the country I'm entering.

To meet these goals, I take the time and effort to be fully prepared at least an hour before going through customs. Surprisingly, it always takes a little longer than I expect.

That's why I often do most of my preparations the day before, and it's why I have a section in our Boat Notebook dedicated to getting us through customs.

For you to prepare for customs, I'd advise you to make sure you've got:

- Your paperwork in order.
- Your estimated time-of-arrival calculated for the customs station for the country you're entering.
- A list of items you'll be declaring when entering the country.
- A pen and paper ready to write information on.
- An accurate and complete list of phone numbers you'll to call for entering the US from the northern and southern BC coasts, and for entering Canada from Washington State and from Alaska.
- A credit card available in case you need to pay the duty for goods purchased in the country you're leaving.
- A fully charged cell phone along with ear plugs.

Your Paperwork is in Order

As a cruiser going from the US to Canada, or vice versa, the ease with which this transpires depends on many variables: your citizenship status, passports, visas, travel cards (Nexus and CanPass), boat registration, etc. If you have any doubt about your ability to enter either country on your boat, I suggest you actually pick up the phone before you even leave home and call the customs people for the country you'd like to enter. (Canada: 888 226 7277. US: 800 563 5943.)

I tell you this from experience.

When I'd first moved to Anacortes from Southern California. I'd already completed the procedures to obtain a Nexus pass (which I highly suggest you do if you're qualified) and felt confident about going through customs, with one exception. According to the Canadian Border Services website, I was only allowed to bring two bottles of wine into their country. That would have been fine if I was just visiting the Gulf Islands. But I wasn't. In fact we had planned to pass through the Gulf Island without stopping at a town on our way to Desolation Sound.

"What can I do?" I asked the Canadian agent. "We'll want a glass of wine at night, but we'll not be able to replenish our stock."

Very politely, the agent explained to me that I could bring more wine with me, but to bring the receipt and expect to pay duty on the extra bottles. In other words, declaring the extra bottles we brought and using a credit card to pay the duty made everything legal.

Coming back to my point, if you have any questions about your paperwork, call the US or Canadian customs ahead of time so you can straighten out any situations before you leave home.

With that, here are the things you should have organized and accessible at the time you go through customs:

- The names of all people on board (the manifest).
- Their passports, visas, driver's licenses if they have one, birth certificates for minors, and Nexus and/or CanPass cards.
- The reason you and each passenger is traveling, each of your end points, and when each of you expects to return.

- List of pets and copies their licenses and vaccination records, which must be up-to-date.
- The boat owners' boat registration numbers.
- Your boat's documentation and registration numbers.
- Your boat's name, length, design, and builder.
- Your boat's current customs decal number.
- The customs number given to you the last time you went through customs on this particular trip, if any.
- The name of the marina or anchorage you just left, and the name of the customs entry point to which you're headed.
- The time you estimate you'll arrive at a specific customs office (see below).
- A list of items you need to declare (see below).
- A suction-cup clip inside one of your boat's side windows to which you'll clip the paper that lists your boat's custom clearance number.

Estimate Your Arrival Time for Port-of-Entry's Customs Office

When you call customs for either the US or Canada, they're going to want to know where and when they can meet you on your boat. For best results, plan ahead!

First, decide on your port of entry.

If you're entering Alaska from Canada, or vice versa, it's very easy to locate the customs check-in office. It's either Ketchikan, Alaska, or it's Prince Rupert, British Columbia. And all boaters must check in, whether you have a Nexus or CanPass card, or not.

If everyone aboard possesses a Nexus or CanPass card, you need to telephone customs for the country you're entering between 30 minutes to 4 hours before reaching your port-of-entry.

If anyone aboard has neither a Nexus nor CanPass permit, you'll need to drive your boat to one of the entry points listed below, dock, and phone customs.

For the rest of the Inside Passage, there's a long list of marine entry points. You'll find these lists in *Waggoner Cruising Guide,* near the front, under US and Canadian Customs Information.

United States from Canada:

Anacortes, Friday Harbor, Point Roberts, Port Angeles, and Roche Harbor. (See *Waggoner Cruising Guide* or US Customs and Border Patrol website cbp.gov for detailed list)

Canada from Washington State Without Nexus/CanPass:

Bedwell Harbour, Campbell River, Nanaimo, Sidney, Vancouver, Victoria, White Rock. (See *Waggoner Cruising Guide* or Canadian Border Services Agency website cbsa-asfc.gc.ca for detailed list)

Canada from Washington State with Nexus/CanPass:

Bedwell Harbour, Campbell River, Nanaimo, Sidney, Vancouver, Victoria, White Rock.

For Nexus/CanPass only:

Cabbage Island; Montegue Harbour, Galiano Island; Horton and Miners Bays, Mayne Island; Port Browning, North Pender Island, and Ganges Harbour Seaplane Dock, Saltspring Island; and 52 Steps Dock, Ucluelet. (See *Waggoner Cruising Guide* or Canadian Border Services Agency website cbsa-asfc.gc.ca for detailed list)

Second, you only need to estimate when you'll get to your port of entry if you're using Nexus or CanPass. After you calculate the time, remembering to adjust for daylight savings time if necessary, call the Nexus/CanPass numbers and tell them your estimated time of arrival. They will want you to arrive no sooner than 30 minutes and no later than 4 hours.

If you're entering Canada, call the Nexus Telephone Reporting Centre (TRC) at 1 866-99-NEXUS (1-866-996-3987).

If entering the United States via Puget Sound, when you cross the Canada/US border, call Nexus at 1-800-562-5943 (for Puget Sound boat arrivals only). Unless directed by a CBP officer to do so, you do not have to report for an in-person inspection.

Declaring Items When Going Through Customs

Cruising in the Inland Passage means you may end up passing back-and-forth between Canada and the US at least once a season. For Capt. Dave and me, crossing the border happens so frequently it feels like old hat.

For this reason, I've learned a thing or two, which I'd like to pass on to you.

First, tell the truth.

Nothing will ruin a lovely cruise like being caught in a lie by customs. If you have more than the allowed alcohol on board, tell customs. Will you automatically have to pay duty on it? Maybe yes. Maybe no, if you've already told customs you're headed for the Broughtons or farther north. Be ready for either to happen.

Will you have to pay duty on liquor products that are already partially consumed? Probably not, especially if you make it clear that what you have on board is for your own consumption.

Why? Ultimately customs agents in both countries are really trying to keep illegal, unsanitary, unregulated, and unsafe products from entering their countries. Bring the food, tobacco, and alcohol you'll need for your cruise, but don't raise flags by making it look like you're starting a black-market import business.

Second, only answer the questions that are asked of you.

I'll never forget the second time we crossed the border into Canada. I was nervous, and the customs agent in Newfoundland to whom I was talking could tell. Finally he said, "Okay, stop. I want you to take a deep breath."

I took a shallow one.

"No, no," he said. "I want to hear you take a deep breath."

Okay. I took a loud, deep breath.

"Now," he said. "Only answer what I ask you. Nothing more. Nothing less. Got that?"

"Yes," I told him.

And then the rest of the conversation was a breeze. If he asked me a yes/no question, he got a yes or no answer. If he wanted to know how many bottles of alcohol we had on board, I told him how many full ones we had, and how many partially-full ones we had.

After he'd completed his questions, he wished me a good trip, which we had. And I thanked him for his advice, which I have now passed on to you.

Third, declare everything.

I can't believe how this piece of advice has made our customs experience easier.

When I say to declare everything, I don't mean to read off a huge list of items you have on board. I'm saying to repeat this sentence when asked what you have to declare: "We're declaring food, alcohol, and tobacco." If you're bringing firearms or more than ten thousand dollars in cash, then you'd say, "We're declaring food, alcohol, tobacco, cash, and firearms."

After declaring everything like this, will the customs agent ask you for more detail? Perhaps. Perhaps not. Be ready for either to happen.

By visiting the US Customs and Border Patrol website and the Canadian Border Services website just before you leave, you'll have the most recent list of customs restrictions. It's important to check this just before you leave, because some restrictions change from year to year depending on livestock and crop diseases, influenzas, etc.

On these two customs sites you'll probably notice a requirement about labeling raw meats. If you have repackaged raw meat for your freezer, please remember to keep the market's label with the meat. If the meat is cooked, labeling is not necessary.

Visiting the two different websites will also provide you the information you need if you plan to bring firearms into either country, as well as cash.

Document Everything: Write the Information Down

As I suggested earlier in this section, have a dedicated place in your Boat Notebook for all things having to do with customs. In this section keep:

- All the customs, Nexus, and CanPass phone numbers.
- All the registration and documentation information you've compiled.
- Lists of what you've declared.
- Clearance numbers as they're given to you by the agent at end of interview.
- Notes on what you'll want to remember next time you go through customs.

Visible Proof

One other thing you must write down on a separate sheet or paper and in bold marking pen is the clearance number the customs agent will give you when your interview is done. Write it on a sheet of paper large enough for the Coast Guard and Border Patrol to read it from their dinghy and affix it to the inside of one of your side windows so it can be read by a border patrol agent in a dinghy.

If you're an American in Canada, keep this number in your window until you return to the US. If you're a Canadian in the US, keep this number in your window until you return to Canada. If you're an American passing through Canada on your way to Alaska, you'll only need your clearance numbers posted when passing northward through Canada, and then southward again (you'll have a different number for each direction because you'll have gone through Canadian customs twice).

Canadian and US Courtesy Flags

According to the U.S. Power Squadron (USPS.org), when you cruise in foreign waters, your vessel should display a small version of that country's flag, called a courtesy flag, whenever your vessel is displaying your country's flag.

On masted boats, fly the courtesy flag alone on the starboard spreader's outboard signal halyard.

On mastless boats, fly the courtesy flag alone on the bow or on a starboard antenna.

For more information about flag etiquette, visit the US Power Squadron's website usps.org and click "Flags."

For Your Boat Notebook

- List of all registration and documentation numbers for you, your guests and pets, and your boat
- List of customs phone numbers to call
- List of items not allowed or having limitations in each country.

Chapter Seventeen

Preparing to Cruise

The Float Plan

For Your Family and Friends ★ For Better Planning

The idea of creating float plan can maybe feel a bit unromantic if you see yourself vagabonding your way up and down the Inside Passage. But there are some very good reasons for creating one, even if you don't precisely adhere to it. These reasons are:

- Your family and friends know your whereabouts in case of an emergency.
- You'll be prepared for the waters and communities (or lack of) you're traveling through.
- You'll allot your time in each place more effectively.

For Your Family and Friends

While you're gone on an extended cruise, you'll be leaving most of your friends and loved ones behind. If something happens to one of them, you'll want to know in a timely way, and especially if it's one of your children or parents.

Problems arise when your family and friends cannot contact you by email or telephone because you're out in some remote spot north of Cape Caution or in the Broughtons or Desolation Sound, where service is notoriously spotty.

If you have developed a float plan, and given copies to trusted friends and family members, they will be able to estimate where you might be on a specific date, and contact the US or Canadian Coast Guard, which ever has jurisdiction. The Coast Guard will then make announcements over marine radio, asking that you radio them back. When you do, they will relay your family's emergency message. If you don't hear the broadcast, chances are good that another cruiser or two has seen your boat and can advise the Coast Guard about where you might be. Recreational boaters tend to willingly help other boaters in distress or need.

With this in mind, when you create your float plan, include the following:

- All the places you expect to visit in chronological order
- Include estimated dates for each visit.
- Specific people you plan to visit along the way, if any. Include their phone numbers, addresses and email contact information.
- Your vessel's name, brand, style, length
- Names of all people on board, along with all forms of contact information.

NOTE: Many cruisers use the SPOT Personal Tracker to stay connected with friends and family while cruising to provide them with your daily movement and position. For information, go to FindMeSpot.com on the Internet.

For Better Planning

Another reason a float plan will help you is because you'll leave home more prepared for the waters and other challenges you'll meet on your travels.

Earlier in this book, I suggested you decide where you want to cruise. You probably noticed as you scanned through the Inside Passage's various regions that they differed from each other quite a bit. In the Broughtons, you'll find lots of anchorages and marinas (i.e., food and fuel), while in Desolation Sound there are mostly anchorages. Cruising around Seattle will mean you need to be hyper vigilant regarding commercial ship traffic, but while down near Olympia, you're not going to meet much commercial traffic.

To make your float plan, figure how far you want to travel and how long it'll take you to get there. If you're crossing difficult waters like Georgia Strait or Cape Caution, allow for weather days so you won't be tempted to venture out into treacherous waters. The weather always calms down, if you're willing to wait a day or few.

When making your float plan also take into consideration where you'll obtain these necessary things:

Food sources

Note where the markets are located and what can you expect to find in them. Every marina does not have a super market. Every market does not have a liquor and tobacco department.

Medical sources

Note where to find major medical facilities in the area in which you are travelling. Usually the bigger the town, the better the facilities will be.

Fuel sources

Know where these are, especially as you travel north of Nanaimo. Exploring Southeast Alaska by Don Douglass has a complete list of fueling stations all the way to Ketchikan.

Laundry sources

Knowing this helps you plan your wardrobe

Personal care sources – hairdressers, manicurists, massage therapists, spas

Finding these sources can mean a lot on a long cruise

Boat repair sources

This is a great reason to carry a *Waggoner Guide*. It will help you find help out in the middle of nowhere?

Internet access

Know which marinas along your path provide Wi-Fi access.

Mailing and shipping sources

Make a note where you can send and receive mail and parcels.

For Your Boat Notebook

- Print-out of your estimated itinerary
- List of places to find food, medical services, fuel, laundry facilities, personal, boat repair, Internet, and mailing services.

ENJOYING YOUR CRUISE

Chapter Eighteen

Enjoying Your Cruise

Understanding the Waters

Accessing and Understanding Current Information
Wind Against Current ★ Tides
Rapids and Narrows
When Rivers Meet the Sea ★ Lagoons

Before moving to northwest Washington, I lived in Southern California, where we cruised in the tricky waters off the coast. I'd often heard fellow cruisers say, "If you can cruise California's Channel Islands, you can cruise anywhere in the world."

Having cruised along the Inside Passage, I no longer agree with that statement at all. Cruising these northern waters takes learning, practice, and at times, careful planning.

And so my primary motivations when understanding the waters of the Inside Passage are:

- Understanding the effects of weather and tides on the water, and use that knowledge to keep us and

our boat safe, and to have lovely passages from one point to the next.
- Understanding how geography affects our cruising waters and use the knowledge to keep us and our boat safe and comfortable.
- Having on board enough provisions to last us in case we need to hunker down for a few days because of dangerous seas.

Accessing and Understanding Current Information

I'm going to divide this section into two parts. The first part explains how to access and understand tide, current, and weather information. The second part describes how they work together and explains why certain conditions are advantageous to travels while others are not.

Currents

Generally speaking, currents in the PNW change directions four times a day. The flood currents bring water in from the Pacific Ocean, and the ebb currents drain water back into the Pacific Ocean. This happens twice a day, and it loosely corresponds to the tide going up and going back down. I repeat: They loosely correspond. Don't ever trust that because high tide is at noon that the flood will begin reversing at noon. It may be as much as an hour off, or more.

Thus, when I suggest you look at current data, don't make the mistake of thinking tide data are the same thing. They're not.

Another thing to keep in mind is that it's not always predictable which direction a specific area of water will move during a flood or an ebb. The Inside Passage is made up of thousands of islands. During both currents, large amounts of water are being pushed around many large and small islands, which leads to some pretty unexpected shifts in the water's direction.

How can you know about these unexpected directions? Look at your charts. On paper charts, look for long arrows. Flood arrows have feathers at the end, while ebb arrows do not. Just remember that FLOOD has FEATHERS (F = F). On software charts, make sure you've turned on Current Data, and then note the direction and color of the arrows. Usually one color represents flood, while another represents ebb.

Obtaining current information

There are several ways you can obtain current data. On *L'Esprit*, we like to have more than one source for tides and currents because in some locations it's very important to traverse waters at slack water. Good resources for obtaining US and Canadian currents are:

In book form: Fine Edge's *Ports and Passes; Canadian Tides and Currents*, from Amazon (make sure you get volumes for the areas in which you'll be cruising).

On the Internet: Google "Canadian Current Tables" and Google "US Current Tables." The Internet current tables for Canada and the US are for specific locations, rather than for areas. Obviously this is not as efficient as having all the year's data in one book.

From navigation software: Most good navigation software has the ability to show you the tides and currents for the area you are in (Garmin, Nobeltec, Rose Point, etc.).

From phone and tablet apps: AyeTides, MyTide, Boating US & Canada.

A word about redundancy

Not only is it important to have multiple sources for current information, it's also important to have multiple brains thinking about current.

Our Fidalgo Yacht Club friends, the Schutzlers, gifted us with a piece of golden advice when we first started cruising in Puget Sound. They advised:

Before you go through any waters where rough currents can impact your safety and comfort, both of you should independently figure the exact times and speeds. If, when you share your calculations, they are the same, you've probably calculated correctly. If not, recalculate until you both agree.

I'm still shocked by how many times Capt. Dave and I have come up with different answers and have had to go back and refigure. The extra time taken refiguring saved us a lot of trouble. And once, as you'll read in a few pages, we didn't refigure and found ourselves in very dangerous waters.

Thus, if you plan to cruise PNW waters affected by currents (just about everywhere), I urge you and your Captain to learn how to find, read, and understand current data. I've already told you where to find current data. Here's what you need to know:

Know the current activity for the entire day.

Both flood and ebb currents last about six hours, generally speaking. Sometimes they're shorted, and sometimes they're longer, but generally they last around six hours.

There are generally four currents per day.

Make it a point to keep in your awareness when the waters will be flooding and ebbing throughout the day. This knowledge will help you when you're driving with and against the current, and when you're arriving at and leaving a dock.

Be aware of the current's direction for all waters you'll be cruising

When you're cruising south of Juan de Fuca Strait, flood currents generally travel south, and ebbs travel north.

When cruising in the southeast side of Vancouver Island up to the vicinity of Middlenatch Island, flood currents generally travel north, and ebbs travel south.

If cruising along the northeast side of Vancouver Island from Middlenatch Island and northward, the flood currents travel south, and the ebbs travel north.

When cruising in Alaska and Canada's Central and Northern Coasts, check your charts for flood and ebb directions. Waters will generally move in the most unobstructed directions for flood and ebb. Again, check your charts for current directions.

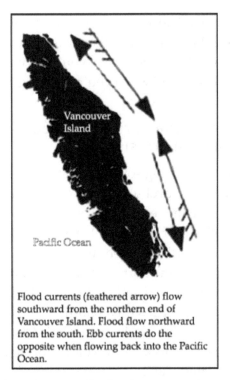

Flood currents (feathered arrow) flow southward from the northern end of Vancouver Island. Flood flow northward from the south. Ebb currents do the opposite when flowing back into the Pacific Ocean.

Know the times of slack current

Throughout any given day, the current will change directions three or four times. The intervals between these changes in direction are called slack, because the water is not being pulled in one direction or the other for a nominal period of time. The water is slack and therefore calm.

There are times, which you'll soon read about, when you'll only want to venture into a body of water during slack, because that's the safest time.

Whichever reference you use for current data, know how to quickly access the exact time of slack.

Current information is usually provided in two ways: as a table and as a line graph.

Current tables

Current table publications provide current data in table form. Some navigation and current apps give current information this way also. In the table below, slack is also referred to as Turn Time.

Day	Turn Time	Max Time	Max Knots
2	4:39 AM	8:05 AM	-6.7
2	11:12 AM	1:51 PM	6.6
2	4:50 PM	8:11 PM	-6.7
2	11:13 PM	2:03 AM	7.3
2	4:39 AM	8:05 AM	-6.7

On the above day, the second day of a month, the current came to a stop (slack) and TURNED directions four times: at 4:39 AM, at 11:12 AM, at 4:50 PM, and at 11:13 PM.

You can also tell that the TURN at 4:39 AM was a turn-to-ebb (from flood) because of the negative sign on -6.7 knots.

From the first line of the table, you can see that the flood tide stopped at 4:39 AM and turned-to-ebb, and that it reached its maximum speed of -6.7 knots at 8:05 AM.

The second line tells you that the ebb current that started at 4:39 AM came to a halt and turned to flood at 11:12 AM. The new flood current reached its maximum speed of 6.6 knots at 1.51 PM. You can also see that the ebb current that started at 4:39 AM lasted 6 hours and 43 minutes (4:39 AM to 11:12 AM is 6:39 or 399 minutes). This is important to know, as you'll soon learn.

This third line tells you that the flood that started at 11:12 AM stopped and turned-to-ebb at 4:50 PM. This new ebb reached its maximum speed of -6.7 knots at 8:11 PM. The whole flood current that started at 11:12 AM and ended at 4:50 PM lasted 5 hours and 38 minutes, or 338 minutes.

The fourth line tells you that the ebb that started at 4:50 PM stopped and turned-to-flood at 11:13 PM. The new flood current reached its maximum speed of 7.3 knots at 2:03 AM (the next morning). The whole ebb current that started at 4:50 PM and ended at 11:13 PM lasted 6 hours and 23 minutes, or 383 minutes.

The last line tells you that the flood that started at 11:13 PM stopped and turned-to-ebb at 4:39 AM. The new ebb current reached its maximum speed of -6.7 knots at 8:05 AM. The whole flood that started at 11:13 PM and ended at 4:39 AM the next morning lasted 5 hours and 26 minutes, or 326 minutes.

Line graphs

Line graphs look like bell curves. The vertical axis has the current's speed, and the horizontal axis will have the time of day. Find 0 knots (slack) on the left. Then move your finger across 'til you find the time when it's 0 knots. That's when slack is.

The First Mate's Guide to Cruising the Inside Passage

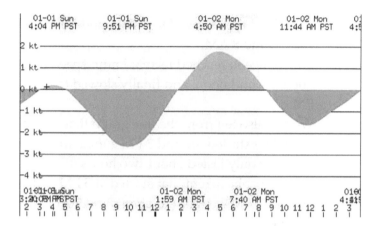

Moving left to right on the above graph, you can tell the following:

- At approximately 3 PM on Jan. 1, the ebb current slacked and turned-to-flood. You know this because the graph line crossed over 0 knots at 3 PM. You know it had been an ebb current because the line was below the zero and in negative territory.
- At approximately 4 PM, the flood current hit its maximum speed of .2 knots. This is a very weak current.
- Around 5 PM, the flood current slacked and turned-to-ebb. You see the line cross the zero at that time and heading into negative territory.
- That new ebb current then reached its maximum speed of -2.6 knots around 10 PM.
- The ebb current finally slowed to slack and turned-to-flood around 2 AM the next morning.
- The new flood reached its maximum speed of 1.75 knots around 5 AM.

203

- That flood then slowed to a slack and turned-to-ebb around 8 AM.
- That new ebb reached its maximum speed of 1.6 knots around noon, and finally slowed to slack at 4 PM.
- We can also tell from the line graph that the first flood that started around 3 PM ended around 5 PM, so it only lasted about two hours.
- The next ebb current that started at 5 PM ended around 2 AM, so it lasted about 8 hours, or 480 minutes.
- The next flood that started at 2 AM ended around 8 AM, so it lasted about 6 hours, or 360 minutes.
- The last ebb current that started at 8 AM ended at 4 PM, which was another 8-hour current, or 480 minutes.

Know the maximum velocities of each flood and ebb current

As you can see from the above examples, each current, whether flood or ebb, starts from slack, begins moving slowly, builds up speed, and then loses steam as it heads toward slack. It usually does this in a span of five or six hours, but some can last longer and some can be shorter. Some currents can gain very little speed, while others can reach speeds up to fifteen knots!

You'll want to know current speeds because they can affect your boat's speed and maneuverability, as well as the sea state if the wind is blowing over ten knots. A four-knot current going against you can slow down your boat considerably. A four-knot current pushing you forward can also seem uncomfortable because a rudder is designed to have water flow over it from the bow.

Navigation and tides-and-currents software programs give you maximum speeds. Click the CURRENTS icon and find the information for the day you're interested in. Some programs tell you outright what the maximum speed of the each current, and when it occurs. Study each source of current information that you'll have on board so you feel comfortable gathering information.

Know in which phase the moon is

You'll also want to always have in mind which phase the moon is in for the day. During a new moon and a full moon (spring tides), there is significantly more water moving into and out of the Inside Passage than during neap tides. Because more water is passing through, it has to move faster. That speed increase can sometimes amount to double the amount of a neap current's velocity. If you're going through notorious rapids or narrows, i.e. Dent Rapids, or making a major crossing, i.e., going around Cape Caution, you'll want to avoid making those passages at the peak of a spring tide, especially if the weather is unsettled.

You'll also see more logs and debris in the water during spring tides. Because more water is pulled into the Inside Passage, the tide rises. Debris on shore is picked up by this tide and taken back out to sea.

The moon's phases can be found in tides-and-currents books that marine stores often give away for free. You can also find the phases online. Just Google "Moon Phases 2016" (or whatever year it is), print the information and put it in your Boat Notebook.

Joanne Wilshin

Estimate a current's speed at any time during its cycle

Obviously if you have navigation software that gives you bell curve of the current's speed and timing, this is easy. But if, for whatever reason you don't have this available to you, you'll want to know how to estimate a currents speed, especially when going through narrows and rapids.

Kevin Monahan's *Local Knowledge* describes a fast way to estimate current speed. Let's just say that slack is at 6:45 AM, and the next slack is at 11:45 AM, which is a 5-hour current. The current reached a maximum speed of 8 knots.

FIRST, calculate the minutes between two slacks (i.e., 300 minutes).

SECOND, divide that by six (300/6=50 min.).

THIRD, note the time of the earlier slack (i.e. 6:45 AM.) and the highest current speed (8 kt.).

FOURTH, apply the "Rule of Sixths" by estimating that current speed reaches 50% of its maximum speed by the first sixth, 90% by the second sixth, 100% by the third sixth, 90% by the fourth sixth, 50% by the fifth sixth, and 0% (slack) by the sixth sixth. Thus the current speeds would be:

0645 = 0 kt.
0735 = 4 kt. (0645 + 50=0735; 50% of 8 kt. = 4 kt.)
0825 = 7.2 kt. (0735 + 50=0825; 90% of 8 kt. = 7.2 kt.)
0915 = 8 kt. (0825 + 50=0915; 100% of 8 kt. = 8 kt.)
1005 = 7.2 kt. (0915 + 50=1005; 90% of 8 kt. = 7.2 kt.)
1055 = 4 kt. (1005 + 50=1055; 50% of 8 kt. = 4 kt.)
1145 = 0 kt. (1055 + 50=1145; 0% of 8 kt. = 0 kt.)
(NOTE: at 0645+25=0710, est. current=2 kt.)

You can also estimate that if the current's traveling 4 knots at 7:35, that it'll be around 2 knots halfway between 6:45 and 7:35 (7:10 AM).

Wind Against Current

All you really need to know about wind against current is:

- When the wind and the current are moving in opposing directions, waves, including standing waves, can occur. In other words, if the current is moving northward, while the wind is blowing southward, standing waves can develop.
- The faster the wind and the faster the current, the higher those waves are.

This is why I've suggested you make large crossings when the wind and the current are mild. You'll decrease your chances of getting caught in rough water.

Tides

You'll want to pay attention to tides when you're:

- Anchoring
- At dock but have a lot of provisioning to do.
- Going through narrows.

When you're anchoring, note where in the tide cycle you are by referring to your navigation software or to your tide-tables booklet. If you're anchoring at low tide, you'll want to know how much higher the tide will rise so you put out enough anchor rode. If you're anchoring at high tide, you'll want to know how much lower the tide will go so you can be sure you won't touch the bottom or won't end up closer to shore or other boats than you want to be.

When you're at a dock and have a lot of provisioning to do, you'll want to do the most toting at high tide. Why? That's when the gangway is the least steep. The lower the tide goes, the steeper the gangway gets.

When you're going through narrows (i.e., Dodd Narrows), you want to traverse when the passageway is more full of water than when it is not. Please read this next section for a clearer picture of what you're looking for when traversing narrows.

Rapids and Narrows

Rapids and narrows are areas of extreme turbulence at maximum current flow. This is a list of the Inside Passage's most notorious rapids and narrows, moving from south to north:

Puget Sound: Tacoma Narrows, Deception Pass Bridge

Gulf Islands: Active Pass, Porlier Pass, Gabriola Pass, Dodd Narrows

Jervis Inlet: Malibu Rapids

Discovery Islands: Seymour Narrows, Serge Narrows, Hole in the Wall, Okisollo Channel

Between Desolation Sound and the Broughtons: Yuculta Rapids, Gillard Passage, Arran Rapids, Dent Rapids, Greenpointe Rapids, Whirlpool Rapids

The Broughtons: Chatham Channel, Stuart Narrows, Kenneth Passage

BC's Northern Coast: Nakwakto Rapids, Draney Narrows, Jackson Pass, Meyers Passage, Grenville Channel, Hawkins Narrows

SE Alaska: Sergius Narrows, Wrangell Narrows, Rocky Pass.

In all of the above waters, and for the most comfortable ride, you'll want to check your tides-and-currents data to travel at the best times.

When going through short narrows, it's most ideal to travel at high slack and during a neap tide. The water is the most calm at that time. Actually, you'll probably find the waters are pretty calm even fifteen minutes before and after slack, which should give you plenty of time to make your passage.

When travelling through long narrows (Grenville), it's most ideal to do the first half going against a dying current when less water is pushing against you, and do the last half traveling with the newly building current.

When travelling through the long stretch of Wrangell Narrows, start going with the dying flood current, and then catch the new building flood current that will be going in the opposite direction. This sounds confusing, but here's the explanation. Remember how flood tides flow around Vancouver Island coming from both the north and south, kind of like fingers and a thumb wrapping around a ball? And the water ebbs back into the Pacific like fingers and a thumb letting go of a ball. Well, Wrangell Narrows is the same. During a flood, water flows south from the north end and it flows north from the south end, like fingers and a thumb wrapping around Mitkof Island. When it ebbs, it flows south from the south, and north from the north.

Sailboats and slower-moving cruisers are more affected by the force of an opposing current than a high-powered power boat, which can just increase its throttle and move right through the slog.

When traveling through rapids, your biggest problems will be whirlpools, eddies, and upwellings. If you plan to go through rapids, please consider reading Kevin Monahan's *Local Knowledge*. He explains how to drive through rapids in order to experience the most safety and comfort.

If you're cruising from Georgia Strait to the Broughtons, you will have to go through rapids. There's no way around it. Ideally, you take these rapids during a neap tide, in fair weather, during the slack between two currents, and between sunup and sundown. Do not even consider going through Dent Rapids at any time other than slack. People's lives have been lost doing that. But if you go at slack, it's a piece of cake.

Read *Waggoner Cruising Guide* for specific information about the waters you'll be traveling through.

When Rivers Meet the Sea

If you're traveling in large water (i.e., Georgia and Queen Charlotte Straits), and you are near a large river or inlet (i.e., Frazier River, Jervis Inlet, Slingsby Channel, Smith Inlet) know that their inflows and outflows will affect you, sometimes quite a bit. Here's what you'll want to keep in mind:

- Usually these rivers and inlets are more comfortable when the current flows up them, than when water is flowing back out.
- Inflows and outflows are more extreme during spring tides.

- Usually the further you are from the actual entry to the river or inlet the better.
- The same rules for wind against current apply to rivers and inlets.

Read *Waggoner Cruising Guide* for more specific information regarding these bodies of water.

Lagoons

My husband loves lagoons. Me, not so much. That's because many lagoons have shallow entries where it's only possible to pass through every six hours. Also, the tide predictions for the area bear little resemblance to the tides for the lagoon. So, you might wonder if we've ever gotten stuck in a lagoon, and the answer would be: yes, the one in Von Donop Inlet in Desolation Sound. In order to get out, Davy went ashore and used lines to pull the dinghy, in pretty much the same way Sal the mule pulled boats through the Erie Canal. My job was to fend us off the piles of rocks boulders along the shore. I was not thrilled.

My suggestion if you want to explore lagoons is to either do it by kayak, or have a very high-powered dinghy you take in while the tide is still high.

Resources

- Fine Edge's *Ports and Passes*
- *Canadian Tides and Currents*, from Amazon (make sure you get volumes for the areas in which you'll be cruising).
- On the Internet: Google "Canadian Current Tables" and Google "US Current Tables."

- Apps: AyeTides, MyTide, Boating US & Canada.

Chapter Nineteen

Enjoying Your Cruise

Navigating the Waters

Creating a Route ★ Following a Route
Right of Way ★ Navigation Aids
Locks ★ Obstacles
Rapids and Narrows ★ Following Seas
Open-Ocean Passages ★ Big City Cruising

Now that you know how the waters of the Inside Passage are affected by weather, tides, and geography, let's think about actually navigating from place to place.

The primary things motivating me whenever we navigate from one place to the next are:

- Being prepared for all the predictable variables in our path.
- Having alternatives to our planned route, just in case.
- Having a safe and comfortable passage as well as finding a good spot to anchor or dock.

Joanne Wilshin

Creating a Route

On *L'Esprit*, we always create a route, even if we don't adhere to it exactly. Capt. Dave usually creates the route on Nobeltec, which is loaded on our boat's laptop. In doing so, he becomes aware of:

- Navigational hazards in our path.
- The direction and time of currents and tides.
- Length and time of the trip.

As First Mate, I usually take a look at the route on the computer, but I also study it in one or more of the following:

- A paper chart for the areas through which we'll be traveling.
- *Marine Atlas* Vol. 1 and 2 (Vol. 2 is my favorite).
- Fine Edge Publication's laminated fold-out charts with anchorage information on the back for the areas we'll be cruising.
- *Waggoner Cruising Guide* for anchoring and docking possibilities.
- At least one more good resource regarding anchorages, such as one of the Dreamspeaker series or the Douglass series for the pertinent area.

Obviously, we don't make this route five minutes before we leave. Whether we're out cruising for months at a time or just taking a day trip, we usually make tomorrow's route decisions the day before. This way we both have a chance to look for things that might concern us and then have a conversation about those things. Sometimes these concerns cause us to change our route in some way or to delay our passage; sometimes we decide the concern is really not a problem at all.

Some of the concerns that can pop up are:

- Is wind predicted to move in the opposite direction from the current? Remember, wind against current, can create uncomfortable sea conditions such as standing waves.
- Are the wind and current predicted to move against your intended direction? This can slow you down, depending on the velocities of the wind and current.
- Is the wind predicted to be greater than 15 knots? As former sailors, a 15-knot wind is not the obstacle that it might be for a powerboat. And not all 15-knot winds are alike. Know what you and your boat can handle.
- Is Fog or heavy rain predicted? If so, you might want to wait a day. Or, if you have radar, you'll venture out with the knowledge that you may need to move more slowly in the water, and that you may have to make course changes to avoid unexpected obstacles.
- Are there rapids or narrows that require precise timing to keep us safe and comfortable?
- Are there rocks, reefs, military exercise areas, shipping and ferry lanes, or expected turbulent waters in our route's path?
- Are there weather buoys and stations surrounding our route that can give us pertinent information regarding the sea state and wind>

- Are there alternate (Plan B) locations for possible docking or anchoring if for some reason our route has to be cut short?

Following a Route

Once the route is agreed upon, gather up all that you'll need to execute the route: charts, books, and weather and current information.

The reason I suggest you gather this information the day before is that often the best time to make some passages is early in the morning. And by early, I mean 00:DARK:EARLY (first light!). The wind and waters are usually pretty tame then. If you'll be leaving at dawn, you will want to have everything gathered up the night before. If you're leaving later in the day, you can obviously hold off packing everything up until the next morning.

When following your route, you'll want to stay pretty true to your course. Sometimes you'll realize you can cut corners, and there's no reason why you shouldn't, as long as you watch for obstacles and shallow depths along the short cut.

For sure there will be events that will force you to alter your route, at least for a time. If you are in danger of colliding with or obstructing a large ship, a ferry, a tug-and-barge combination, a working boat, or a commercial fisherman, you need to get out of their way. Make it abundantly clear that you will stay out of their way by: 1) noticeably changing your course and/or 2) calling them up on the radio and asking what they'd like you to do OR telling them your intentions. Do not assume they will alter their course for you. In many cases their inability to maneuver gives them legal right-of-way.

Rules of the Road

As First Mate, learn the right-of-way rules, or at least have the rules easily accessible. You never know when you'll be in full charge of your boat while underway.

In general, as the operator of a boat, you're responsible for:

- Operating your boat safely. In other words, watch your wake and speed, proactively avoid collisions, drive sober, go where you can see, and don't endanger others or their property.
- Avoiding military areas and other areas restricted by Canada's and the US's security departments, such as dams, bridges, power facilities, etc.

You're also responsible for knowing where your boat falls in the pecking order that determines who has the right-of-way in any given circumstance. The pecking order is (from highest degree of right-of-way, to the least):

- Unmanned vessels (i.e., boats at anchor).
- Difficult-to-maneuver boats (i.e., large ships and tugs with barges).
- Deep-drafted boats which have limited areas in which to maneuver.
- Commercial fishing vessels that are fishing.
- Row boat.
- Boats under sail.
- Boats under power.
- A seaplane before it lands.

By looking at the above list, I'm guessing you can think of some instances when it's not entirely clear who has right-of-way. For example, does a:

- Sailboats under sail and power have priority over a power boat? No, because it has it's motor on.
- Sailboats under sail have priority over a power boat towing another boat? Probably not, because of maneuverability.
- Sailboats under sail always have priority over a fishing boat heading out to its fishing grounds? No, because it's not fishing.
- Tugboats always have priority over other sail and power boats? No, only when it's towing or powering a barge.

The three main instances you'll need to follow right-of-way rules are when:

- You are overtaking another vessel
- When you are crossing in front of another vessel from left to right, or vice versa.
- When you are heading directly into the path of another vessel.

For the above instances, you'll need to follow these rules:

Overtaking a vessel

If you are overtaking another vessel from behind, it's your responsibility to stay out of its way.

If the boat you're overtaking requests you not to overtake it, you must oblige.

To ask a boat to pass it, make two short horn blasts, or radio them. They'll either say yes or make two short horn blasts, or they'll say no or make five short blasts.

Crossing in front of a vessel

If there is a danger that you might collide with the boat you're crossing in front of, obey the right-of-way rule.

The vessel on the right has right-of-way, period. If you look out your bow, and the other boat is on your right, you have to take its rear. If you look out your bow, and the other boat is on your left, you have right of way.

If you can't tell if you might collide, put it to the constant-bearing-decreasing-range (CBDR) test. The constant-bearing-decreasing-range rule states that if you keep looking at an approaching vessel from a specific angle, and its bearing doesn't change to the left or right, you're going to collide. Eek!

Here's how to do the CBDR test: 1) Remain seated in comfortable a stationary position. 2) Point directly at the other vessel and freeze. 3) Remember the exact position your hand and arm are in. 4) Re-enact that position once a minute.

If, each time you re-enact that position, you're always pointing at the other boat, you'll eventually collide with it. Either slow down, speed up, radio them if you have right-of-way, or change course. When the other boat moves to the left or right of your hand, the danger has passed. Remember if a collision is imminent, avoid it, even if you have the right of way. Better to be right than dead right.

Heading directly into another boat's path

If it looks like you might collide, change your course to the right a few degrees. If that's not possible, change to the left a few degrees. But standard procedure is to move to the right.

Right-of-way rules for sailboats

First, get acquainted with what a tack is, with regards to right-of-way.

Starboard tack means the wind is blowing from starboard or right-hand side of your boat, and the wind is pushing your sails toward the port side.

Port tack means the wind is blowing from the port or left-hand side of your boat, and the wind is pushing your sails toward the starboard side.

A **windward vessel** is the boat the wind reaches before the leeward boat. In other words, the windward vessel protects the **leeward vessel** from the wind.

An **uncertain tack** is one where you really can't tell from which side the wind is coming. Uncertain tacks can be see when spinnakers are flying or when a boat is travelling wing-on-wing (when the jib and mainsail are spread on opposite sides so it looks like flying wings).

If your sailboat and another sailboat, both with your engines off, appear to be on a collision course, please follow these rules:

Different tacks: The starboard tack vessel has right-of-way. (Right tack has right.)

Same tack: The leeward vessel has right-of-way.

Uncertain tack: Port tack has NO right-of-way.

Right or dead right

Always avoid a collision, even if another boat stands on your right-of-way

If you exercise your right-of-way and subsequently experience a collision, you can be found partially at fault.

Driving the Boat

I urge all first mates to learn to drive your boat. For some of you, this may seem like a tall request. Still, I urge to you learn to drive your boat. There will be times when the captain, if he is the usual helmsman, will need you to take over the controls, and you'll want to be helpful. Sometimes such instances are life and death situations, and you'll want to feel that you were of help, rather than a hindrance.

With that in mind, here are some suggestions for becoming a better and more confident boat-driver:

If you have a phobia about driving the boat, start by taking baby steps. Drive in a straight line for three minutes at a time. Then gradually build up your confidence to steering a curve, then slowing the boat to a stop to make a right or left turn, and so on. Every time you take your boat out on the water, give yourself a few minutes to build confidence.

Driving a sailboat is quite different from driving a power boat. And driving a twin engine powerboat is quite different from driving a single engine boat. If you have thrusters, whether on a sailboat or a powerboat, the driving experience will differ from boats that don't. Learn what it takes to drive your boat.

The Internet is full of videos showing how to drive a boat and how to dock a boat. Go on YouTube and type in "How to drive a sailboat," or "How to drive a twin screw (or single screw) powerboat," and you'll see what I mean. The Internet is a goldmine!

Many second mates I know have hired a licensed captain to teach them the ropes. This is a useful idea if it's in your budget. The captain can be aboard, or not, since you're hiring a licensed captain. Regardless, the captain doesn't have to be hovering over you while you learn, which for some people makes learning easier.

Ultimately, you'll want to be able to drive your boat to a destination and stop it there. If it's a bay or cove, it's easier then coming to a dock. Find yourself a spot to anchor, and do so. If, however, you're coming to a dock, and your captain is indisposed, you'll want to call the dock first, tell them your predicament, and ask for assistance when you get there. You might want to ask for a dock, rather than a slip. Then you'll want to drive very slowly toward the dock when you know someone will be there to help you. It doesn't have to be pretty or perfect. In fact, I've had conversations with fellow first mates who usually do not drive their boat into the slip, and we've all said the same thing: "I know I can get the boat to the dock, but it won't necessarily be quiet or pretty." What's the saying? Any landing's a good landing.

Driving a boat is like a car in that it requires small changes in direction when traveling in a relatively straight line. Making big wheel turns, as you might see in a Hollywood movie, will cause your boat to make big direction changes. When driving in a straight line, make small corrections and then wait for the boat to settle out before making more corrections. Just a suggestion!

A great little driving exercise

When we first got *L'Esprit*, a friend gave us a magazine article that described some boat-driving exercises designed to give us a better feel for how our boat handled. I have no idea where to find the article for you, but I do remember what it asked us to do. It asked us to find a buoy or mark out in the water. We were to drive in a large and a small circle around the buoy in both directions. Then we were to drive around the buoy in a box shape, in both directions. In other words, we had to drive straight, stop the boat and make a ninety-degree turn, then drive straight, and then make another ninety-degree turn, and so on. Then we had to do it driving in reverse, going both clockwise and counter-clockwise. Obviously this took time, but it gave both of us a great feel for how to handle our boat. I highly recommend it for you if you want to improve your skills.

Navigation Aids

While there are definite similarities to Canadian and US navigation aids (buoys, lights, cans, day marks), I would consider downloading and/or printing their regulations and keep them on your boat.

You can access the American rules by going to USCGBoating.org/images/486.PDF and downloading "US Aids to Navigation: What You Need to Know About the Markers on the Water."

For "The Canadian Aids to Navigation System 2011," Google its title.

The US Coast Guard publishes a book titled *Navigation Rules and Regulations Handbook*, which you can purchase on Amazon in either paper or Kindle version. If your boat is 12 meters or longer, you are required to carry a copy of this book on board.

If you are taking a long cruise into wilderness areas, I would also suggest you have on board a copy of Nigel Calder's *How to Read a Nautical Chart*. On our trip to Alaska, we found we needed to refer to it more than a few times because of chart markings we knew nothing about.

Some navigational aid basics you most boaters will assume you know are:

When coming from seaward, green lights, green signs, and odd numbers are on the left or port side of the channel. Stay to the right of these marks.

When coming from seaward, red lights, red signs, and even numbers are on the right or starboard side of the channel. Stay to their left.

When going back out to seaward, everything is the opposite. Red and even numbers will be on the left. Green and odd numbers will be on the right.

An easy way to remember this is to memorize the saying, "Red right returning." In other words, when returning from seaward, red (and even numbers) will be on the right.

Locks

If your cruising grounds include Puget Sound, there may be a chance you'll be going through the Ballard Locks, also known as the Hiram M. Chittenden Locks. The locks connect the very popular and busy Lakes Union and Washington with Shilshole Bay and the rest of Puget Sound.

There are a lot of things to be aware of the first time or two you go through the locks. There are also plenty of

YouTube videos that show what you might expect when going through.

First of all, here's some general information.

- There are two locks, one smaller than the other.
- The western entry/exit is at Salmon Bay, and the eastern entry/exit is at Lake Washington Ship Canal.
- Lake Washington Ship Canal is crossed by seven bridges: two fixed and five draw or bascule. The bridge tenders monitor channels 13 and 16.
- Two good publications to help you with lock specifics are *Waggoner Cruising Guide* and NOAA's Booklet Chart 18447 (found on-line). You'll learn the exact heights and names of the bridges, as well as other helpful information.
- The speed limit when entering the lock is between two-and-a-half and three knots.
- You never really know which one you'll be going through until you get there.
- There will be pedestrians watching you go through the locks because you are on the sightseeing list for Seattle visitors. Wear clothing.
- There will be lock workers taking your lines.

Before going through the locks, you should have the following equipment on deck and ready for deployment:

- Two 50-foot mooring lines, each with a 12-inch (in diameter) eye splice at one end. If you go through the small lock, 30-foot lines are fine.
- Plenty of fenders for both sides of you boat.

Joanne Wilshin

When you go through the locks from either the eastern or western entrance, you'll be:

- Travelling as a pack with other boats going in the same direction you'll be going.
- If you're in the large locks, don't be surprised if you travel with some large commercial vessels, though not the size of tankers.
- You'll be waiting outside the locks until they open the gates, at which time the group of vessels coming from the opposite entrance will head toward you as they go on their way. Sometimes it gets a little testy when everyone's outside waiting, especially if there is a lot of traffic. Boaters are worried they won't get in with the group, etc. Try to remain calm.
- When it's your turn to enter, you'll see a green light. Commercial and government boats will be loaded first. Enter slowly.
- Be prepared to raft either to the starboard or port.
- Whoever drives your boat into the locks should stay at the controls until the boat is securely tied.
- A lock operator will tell you where to go, and will take lines. In the large locks, give the lock operator the eye end of your line. In the small locks, put the eye end around your cleat and hand the lock operator the line end, which he'll return to you to cleat off.
- If you are on the edge, you will be handing lines to the lock operator. Be prepared for another boat to raft up to you. Also be prepared to raft to another boat and not the wall. (See Ch. 21)

- When a dock operator gives you instructions, repeat those instructions out loud.
- Try to be calm and follow directions. You may find yourself in locks with as many as a hundred boats.
- Keep an eye on your lines, especially when the water level is dropping. If your lines are too tight, loosen them. Otherwise you might find yourself dangling.
- Just before the locks open, you may be asked to make your lines more secure because of the current.
- Release your lines only after the lock operators ask you to do so.
- When casting off, untie the lines nearest the saltwater first, and the ones closest to freshwater last.

Obstacles

While underway anywhere in the Inland Passage, you will no doubt run into one or more of the following obstacles:

Trees, logs, deadheads, and snags

During spring tides (around the full and new moons), high tides will capture trees from shore and take them out to sea. This explains why sometimes you'll meet a slew of logs and debris for miles at a time. Sometimes this is exasperated when there has been a recent landslide or a commercial log boom has broken.

Avoid hitting trees and logs. They will destroy your running gear. If you find yourself in a thicket of logs, it's best to idle your way through. The logs will move to the side without destroying your spinning propeller. Note: if you see a line of birds standing on the water's surface, they're probably on a log. Avoid them.

Always be on the lookout for deadheads, which are mostly-submerged root balls or upright logs floating in the water. They can be lethal to your running gear.

Snags are stationary logs or trees found in the water that are somehow stuck to the sea bottom. Sometimes thoughtful mariners tie floats to these anomalies to help others avoid them. Snags are one reason we avoid passing over innocent-looking shallow rises we see on our charts. You never know what can be stuck on the top of one of those.

Landslides

Sometimes in anchorages surrounded by steep mountainsides an abundance of rain will cause a landslide. It doesn't happen often, but it does happen. In Alaska, earthquakes can cause landslides too. Keep this in mind when anchoring in a cove. Don't just look at the water depth. Scan the mountainsides too.

Tsunamis

Tsunamis are rare, but they happen. We've never been around for one, but we met a couple who were cruising Southeast Alaska for the tenth time. Based on their past experience, they advised us to always keep a radio on to channel 16 in case there is a tsunami advisory. They explained that one year they heard just such an advisory while in a cove nestled on the west side of Baranof Island. They had to weigh anchor and go out to sea a ways to avoid getting caught in the incoming tide. Fortunately, it was a false alarm. But they were glad they'd head the advisory in the first place.

Animal life

It's fun to see wildlife while cruising, but there are a few things you should keep in mind.

Whales and orcas are huge, and sometimes they'll appear out of nowhere. Canada and the US have laws generally requiring you to stay at least 200 yards away from a whale and to idle your engine. Don't swim with or feed whales. For more information, you can check out BeWhaleWise.org.

Stellar sea lions are huge, sometimes three times the weight of a grizzly bear. Slow down when you see one swimming around you. And don't be tempted to swim around one!

Jellyfish are a pain in the neck. The Inside Passage is rife with Moon Jellyfish, which don't sting. Instead, they'll clog up your intake valves. If you find yourself cruising where there's been a lot of these jelly fish, check your intake filters often to avoid overheating later on.

Visual difficulties

Fog, rain, and glaring sunlight can make seeing where you're going on the water difficult. Even driving through placid water that perfectly reflects the surrounding landscape can imperil your visibility.

In these times, slow down and make sure you have two sets of eyes on the road. Turn on your radar if necessary.

Sudden shallows

I consider places where the sea bottom suddenly rises to be navigational hazards. You never know if a tree or something has floated along and gotten lodged on one of these sea mounts. If the water under us is less than twenty feet or six meters, we don't drive over it. If we have no choice but to drive over it, we do so at a reduced rate.

Float planes

You'll see a lot of float planes all along the Inside Passage. If you're anchored in a bay and see a float plane heading your way, know that it has the responsibility to avoid colliding with you. When landing, float planes do not have right-of-way. It is only when they actually land that they have to abide by mariners' right-of-way rules. However, the most important rule for all mariners to follow is to avoid collisions. So try to be predictable when around float planes. Help float plane pilots easily calculate what you'll do next.

Crab and prawn traps

Crab and prawn pots can be found in the most unexpected places along the Inside Passage. Always be on the lookout for them. Crab pots usually have a colorful, oblong float attached to them. A bright, round ball float identifies prawn pots. Often there will be a string of pots, instead of one single trap.

Crab and prawn pots should have a weighted line connecting the pot to its float. Sometimes this is not the case. Steer clear of these pots so you don't get these lines caught in your running gear, which can be expensive to repair.

Fishing boats and their gear

According to mariners' right-of-way rules, sailboats and powerboats must give priority to commercial fishing boats while they are fishing.

You also have to avoid all their fishing gear. How you do that is explained here:

Purse Seiners are large fishing boats that have a heap of netting on their stern, but no large spool. They will drop one end of the net in the water. Attached to this end is a large, bright, ball. They will then drive in a large circle, letting out the net. When they reach the ball at the start of the net, they tie it all up. Ultimately, they are a boat with a large circle-shaped net fence off their rear. Your job is to avoid all that and to not cause problems for them with your wake.

Gillnetters are fishing boats with a large spool of netting on their stern. The end of the net that they let out first has a large, bright-red ball float tied to it. After letting out this end, they travel in a straight path as they let out the rest of the line. Your job is to avoid the whole length of line and to not disrupt the operation with your wake.

Trollers have two long booms sticking up and outboard near their stern. These booms are like huge fishing rods: long, hooked-and-baited lines lead from the booms and into the water. Your job is to steer clear of these lines and not interrupt the fishing operation in any way.

Trawlers look similar to purse seiners because they don't carry a large spool nor do they have booms angled outward like huge fishing poles. They are similar to seiners in that they let out a huge, netted scoop which they trail behind them for an hour or two. Obviously your job is to steer clear of and avoid disrupting this operation.

Crabbers/Prawners are boats that tend commercial crab and prawn pots.

Long Liners are similar to gillnetters in that they let out a long, straight, baited line (instead of netting) which is marked with large, red ball floats. Please avoid these.

Wakes

Boat wakes can be disruptive; ship wakes can be dangerous. Every once in a while we've met a ship's wake that has taken our breath away. We could see them coming from afar, that's how tall they were.

If you're about to meet one, head toward it at a forty-five degree angle and slow down, but don't idle. Since waves lose their strength the longer they last, you can also turn away from it and let it catch you when it's weaker.

One lesson we learned from the first large wake we experienced in our powerboat was that our anchor needed to be tied down in the bow roller because it didn't have a keeper. In other words, when *L'Esprit* hit the wake, the anchor rose up and out of the roller. Fortunately it came right back down in its right spot. If it hadn't, our anchor would have been dangling over the side of the boat. Yikes!

Debris

There are all kinds of debris in the water, from logs and dead heads to dead animals and junk found in current lines. Obviously try to avoid it all, but we all know that's sometimes impossible. Here are some tips:

Logs

If you come upon a bunch of them together, probably because they've broken free of a log boom, put your boat in neutral and float through them.

Fishing traps:

Stay at least six feet away from them. If you can tell which way their lines are tending, go on the opposite side. Watch out for floating lines. They're rare, but you don't want to get one snarled in your propeller. If you accidentally cruise over one, immediately put your boat in neutral.

Litter in a current line:

If you're under sail, you probably have little to worry about. If you're under power, you'll want to take the clearest route or slow down. Do this to avoid sucking stuff up into your through hulls and sea water intake.

Rapids and narrows

Rapids and narrows are all passable at some point each day, even the horridly dangerous ones like Arran and Nakwakto Rapids, and narrows always have three or four times during the day when their currents slow down and become slack. Know exactly when those times are. If the narrows you're travelling through are also quite shallow at low tide, know the times for high tide so you can pass through without hitting bottom.

To help you prepare for rapids and narrows:

- Know your boat's depth. If you have a deep keel or draft, you'll always want to be aware of the water depths you'll be travelling through. We always take into consideration that tree parts can

be snagged on the shallow bottom and opt for travelling when the tide has risen more.
- Know your boat's power capabilities against an adverse current. If you have a lot of power, you'll probably be able to buck a moderately adverse current of say two to three knots. But an adverse current stronger than that can become quite uncomfortable and even dangerous. What you don't want is to travel against a current that is so great that you make no or very little headway. Best wait for a better time.
- Know your boat's steering capabilities when going with a current. When you're going with the current, you lose some of your steering capabilities because the water is flowing over the keel from behind you. In a lightly pushing current this is usually not a problem. But if a current's speed rises above three knots, this can be uncomfortable and unsafe. In wide open waters, a pushing current can make you feel like a leaf on the water. In narrows and rapids, you can feel out of control.
- Know your personal capabilities. Going through rapids and narrows at slack current is usually a breeze. Making the passage at other times can be frightening to some. Know your limitations and your willingness to push your own boundaries.
- Know the depth, current speed and direction, and obstacles you'll be facing in the rapids or narrows you're about to pass through. Don't estimate. Look at the chart for current direction, obstacles, and depth contours. Check your current information.

Know what you'll be meeting before you encounter it.

Read Kevin Moynihan's *Local Knowledge* for detailed instructions about going through whirlpools, eddies, and rapids. When forced to move toward a swirling eddy, approach the side coming at you, rather than the side moving away from you. Better yet, Moynihan's book will show you how to move with the tongue, rather than around eddies.

Consider heeding *Waggoner Cruising Guide*'s advice: Go through rapids and narrows during a neap tide and at the end of a high tide, when more water is in the basin. Remember you can usually go through rapids and narrows fifteen minutes before or after slack. You don't have to go through at exactly slack time.

Also, consider rehearsing your passage if doing it for the first time. Both you and the Captain follow your intended course on both the digital and paper charts you use. Note what you'll meet and when you'll meet it. This is especially helpful advice we got from Sherry and Eric Muller when we were preparing to go through narrows in Alaska like Rocky Pass, Wrangell Narrows, and Sergius Narrows. Their specific advice that really worked on *L'Esprit*, and it may work for you, was when going through complex passages, make a list of all buoys and other marks you'll be passing beforehand, and then check each off as you actually pass it on your passage.

Following Seas

In a sailboat, following seas from the open ocean are often a boon, as long as they're not too close together. In a powerboat they're often more of a problem. When you're making a passage exposed to the Pacific Ocean, always monitor weather buoys to ascertain the wave height and periods between waves.

Generally, if the wave height in feet equals the period in seconds, you'll have an uncomfortable ride (i.e., two-foot waves and two-second period). If the period is one-and-a-half times the wave height, it will be better (two-foot waves and 3 second period), and obviously a period two times greater than the wave height is even calmer (two-foot waves and 4-second period). Also, it is not wise to have the autopilot on when experiencing anything but the mildest of following seas.

Open-Ocean Passages

One of the glories of cruising in the Inside Passage is that most of your cruising will be done in protected waters, or at least fairly protected waters. That said, you will need to venture into the Pacific Ocean if you go north of the Broughtons, around Cape Caution, and into Ketchikan. You will be directly exposed to the Pacific Ocean when cruising west of Whidbey Island and through the Strait of Juan de Fuca, the northern portion of Queen Charlotte Strait, Smith Sound, Rivers Inlet, Seaforth Channel outside of Shearwater, Wright Sound, Chatham Strait (Alaska), Clarence Strait (Alaska), and Cross Sound (Alaska).

Please don't let this deter you. The Pacific Ocean is not a heaving mess on a constant basis. Listen to the weather.

Check applications such as PredictWind and SailFlow. Make your passage when seas are settled (one meter or less), when the weather is helpful, and when you're not at the peak of a spring tide.

Crossing Georgia Strait, some thoughts

Even though the Strait of Georgia is protected from Pacific Ocean, it is a large body of water that reflects the effects of Johnstone Strait to the north, the Frazier River to the southeast, and the weather from everywhere. Because I've had some awful crossings, a couple of years ago I dedicated a summer to having nothing but lovely passages. Here are some things I learned:

- The Strait is usually calmer in the morning, but not always. It all depends on the wind.
- Monitor the weather and water conditions several days before your planned passage date. Are conditions building? Or are they easing? The most comfortable passages are in light winds with the water laid down.
- Listen carefully to the buoys near the end of your passage. If their wind and wind waves are settled, and conditions are not building, it's a good omen for you.
- Know that if the wind has blown from the north through Johnstone Strait the night before, you may experience some lump, even if the wind during your passage is down.
- Always listen for word telling you whether Whiskey-Golf, the military exercise area just northeast of Nanaimo, is open or closed. You're in

luck if it's open. Otherwise you'll have to add time to your trip by going around it. Do not go through it if it is closed. You could experience surprise submarines or non-lethal torpedoes (which sometimes get lost!).
- Seas can get a bit rough around the southern end of Malaspina Inlet when Jervis Inlet and Agamemnon Channel are ebbing. There are bays and coves along the coast in which to find safety (Pender Harbor and Secret Cove).
- Malaspina Inlet is usually calmer early in the morning, rather than in the afternoon when the winds have whipped up.

Some cruisers prefer to traverse the western side of Georgia Strait. After Nanaimo, there are not a lot of places to seek shelter, except for Comox and Tribune Bay on Hornby Island. Also, the winds that can whip down from Qualicum can be nasty, but will pass.

On *L'Esprit*, heading north, we like to depart from Silva Bay on Gabriola Island. From there we head across the strait and go through Welcome Passage east of Thornmanby Island. We then head northward to Pender Harbor, which we think is just lovely. As in Comox, you'll find a supermarket there!

Rounding Cape Caution, some thoughts

Waggoner Cruising Guide explains perfectly how to go around Cape Caution. I would urge you to read it in full, if you're planning to make the passage. From my own experience, I offer these thoughts, which you'll also find in *Waggoner*:

- Cross during a neap tide if possible. Less water is filling up and draining out of the water ways.
- Cross when the wave height at West Sea Otter Buoy is one meter or less. Really. We did not follow this advice on a southward passage to Millbrook Cove in Smith Sound, which is just north of Cape Caution. Sea Otter Buoy reported the wave height to be 2.4 meters. Egg Island Lighthouse, which we'd be passing close by, said the waves were two-feet with a low, westerly swell. Guess which one was right? Yep. West Sea Otter Buoy. We were in the horrible seas West Sea Otter Buoy predicted, and I lost some dishes because of it. Lesson learned. West Sea Otter Buoy < One Meter.
- Stay in deeper water. You'll notice on a chart that the ocean shallows closer to shore when going around Cape Caution. This creates waves, which you don't have to experience if you stay further out. Two-hundred feet is a good depth.
- Stay west of Slingsby Channel (northwestern Queen Charlotte Strait) during an ebb tide, especially a spring ebb. Slingsby Channel shoves a heck of a lot of water back into Queen Charlotte Strait during an ebb tide. When mixed with a northwesterly wind, dangerous standing waves form (remember, wind against current!).

Crossing Dixon Entrance, some thoughts

If you're planning to cross Dixon Entrance to venture into SE Alaska, I'm assuming you have a fair amount of boating experience behind you. Which will be good, since you probably won't balk when I say: Leave when the weather and seas are opportune. Again, *Waggoner* Cruising Guide does a good job of explaining how to cross Dixon Entrance. With that, here are my suggestions:

- Before departing, chart your route.
- Before departing, familiarize yourself with places to duck in should you need to abort your passage.
- US customs requires that you check in at Ketchikan on your way north. Canadian customs requires you check in at Prince Rupert on your way south. If, during your passage, the weather and sea conditions deteriorate to such extent that you feel you are not safe, you may anchor in a cove. You must call the customs to which you are headed and tell them where you are and when you expect to arrive in Ketchikan or Prince Rupert.
- Listen to the weather for days before you plan on crossing in order to sense if the weather is building or calming.

One of the problems of crossing Dixon Entrance is the requirement that you check in to customs when you enter either the US or Canada. The only places you can do this is Ketchikan, AK, or Prince Rupert BC. That means you have quite a ways to travel once you've entered either country. Ketchikan is almost ninety nautical miles from Prince Rupert.

Here are some suggestions to make this easier.

- If you're travelling to Alaska from Canada, consider departing from Brundige Inlet on the north end of Dundas Island, BC, or from Wales Harbour on the northwest end of Wales Island, BC.
- If you're travelling to Canada from Alaska, consider leaving from Foggy Bay or Nakat Bay. There are a few other coves and bays in this general area. Read *Northwest Boat Travel* for good information about these sites.
- If you find yourself in rough seas after you've crossed into the US or Canada, you may duck into a bay for safety. You must, however, call customs for the country you've entered and explain the situation and where you are.

Big-City Cruising

When I say big-city cruising I'm talking about being in the marinas in Seattle, Tacoma, Vancouver, Victoria, Nanaimo, Campbell River, Ketchikan, Juneau, and Sitka.

When in these areas, you'll find yourself near the bottom of the food chain. You're having the time of your life on your pleasure craft, while all around you are working boats of all sorts: fishing boats, ocean liners and ferries, tankers, tugs towing barges, the Coast Guard, float planes, etc. Their drivers' primary focus is on getting their job done. When you get in their way, you are a nuisance. Keep this in mind. By all means:

- Follow the rules of the road.

- Maintain your course and speed.
- If you intend to get out of a working boat's way, make that clear to him by either radioing him or making an obvious course change.
- Keep alert to all vehicles around you. 360 degrees around you.
- Keep your marine radio on. Even better, keep two or more marine radios on.

When visiting a big-city marina, you'll be wise to make a reservation a day or more in advance. Jot down the name of the harbormaster when you make the reservation. Calling people by their names pays dividends in goodwill.

Also before arriving at the marina:

- Read through *Waggoner Cruising Guide and Northwest Boat Travel* for a visual of the marina so you'll understand where you're going when you get your dock assignment. If neither book shows the marina's layout, you'll most likely find it in *The Burgee*. Also, zoom in on your electronic navigation program.
- When you get to the marina, collect guides and maps for restaurants, transportation, markets, etc.
- Peruse *Waggoner* and any other cruising guides you have for special experiences the city offers. If you collected this information from the Internet before you left home, refer to it.
- Know when low and high tides occur. High tides provide the least steep gangways, which low tides make gangways steeper. You'll want to know this

if you're hauling a lot of groceries from the store, or you have tons of laundry to do.
- If there's a supermarket in the marina's town, they'll often give you a lift back to you boat.
- Some marinas in Alaska require your boat to have an isolation transformer, which prevents people from being shocked or electrocuted when going from their boat to the dock, and vice versa. Ask the harbormaster about this in advance so you don't end up having to move to different spots in the marina. I'm telling you this from experience.

Resources

- *How to Read a Nautical Chart*, Nigel Calder
- US Aids to Navigation: What You Need to Know About the Markers on the Water. (USCGBoating.org/images/486.PDF)
- The Canadian Aids to Navigation System 2011" found on the Canadian Coast Guard website.
- Navigation Rules and Regulations Handbook, US Coast Guard

For Your Boat Notebook

- Pages that help you figure tides and currents for specific times and places.
- Information about towns and cities you'll be visiting.

Chapter Twenty

Enjoying Your Cruise

Understanding the Weather

How to Collect and Use Weather Information
Where You are and Where You're Going
Know Locations of Marine Weather Buoys and Lighthouses
Collect Reported Information in a Dedicated Notebook
Decide if Safe Passage is Possible
Short-Cruise Weather Gathering ★Special Situations

For cruisers, weather is crucial to comfort and safety. Obviously. Boating is, after all, an outdoor activity. But more importantly, weather affects sea conditions. It can make our cruising passage sublime, or terrifying. I'd personally rather wait a day at anchor or moorage to wait for the weather to settle down than to venture out in twenty or thirty-knot winds. I have friends who are comfortable going out in those kinds of winds, but they either have a sailboat or they have a heavy trawler-type vessel that fares well in those conditions. In other words, know thyself, and know thy boat's capabilities.

With regard to marine weather, I am motivated by my desire to:

- Have a safe, comfortable passage. I don't get a thrill out of being frightened or being thrown around. But I also know that placid passages are a gift, not a rule. So I know what I'm comfortable with, and what I'm not.
- Be kind to my boat. I really don't like pushing *L'Esprit*'s boundaries out in the middle of who-knows-where. Capt. Dave always says she can take it, which she probably can, but what if he's wrong? See my point?
- Know what lies ahead of us on our passage, so we can plan accordingly.
- Have access to as complete a picture of the weather as we can afford.

How to Collect and Use Weather Information

First of all, I'm going to separate acquiring weather information into two parts: weather for an extended cruise and weather for a short cruise.

Extended-cruise weather gathering

On a long cruise where you'll probably be venturing out into exposed waters and remote locations, you'll need to have a spiral notebook or journal of some sort, or even a white board. The reason for this is that every day of your cruise you'll be collecting weather information a couple of times a day for one or more weather regions. You really can't see weather trends if you write forecasts down on scraps of paper that get easily shuffled.

In your spiral notebook (or whatever you choose to gather information), you'll be collecting whatever information NOAA or Environment Canada airs on the radio. In some cases it may take ten-to-fifteen minutes to hear the entire loop of:

- Current marine synopsis of what's currently happening.
- Marine forecast of what's expected for the rest of the day and tomorrow.
- Extended marine forecast for the next three days.

You'll want to hear the weather at least twice a day. Don't be at all surprised if the forecast unexpectedly changes for the good or bad, and don't ever assume that tonight's prediction for tomorrow morning will automatically be correct when morning arrives. If you're making a big passage, check the weather before you leave.

So, to recap, the trick to collecting and judging the weather is to:

- Know where you are and where you're going.
- Know where the marine weather buoys and lighthouses are located.
- Collect reported information in a dedicated notebook at least twice a day.
- Decide if the forecasted conditions will provide you a safe comfortable passage, or not.

Where You are and Where You're Going

Marine weather radio transmissions are designed to provide you synopses and forecasts for weather in the vicinity where you currently are.

If you're in the Broughtons, for example, you'll not be hearing weather for Olympia, Washington, or for Ketchikan, Alaska.

Instead, you'll hear synopses and forecasts for the Queen Charlotte Strait area, where you are currently located. You'll also hear synopses and forecasts for Georgia Strait area immediately south of you, as well as synopses and forecasts for the Queen Charlotte Sound area, immediately north of you, and for the west coast of Vancouver Island, immediately to the west of you.

Know Locations of Marine Weather Buoys and Lighthouses

When listening to a marine broadcast loop, which repeats continually throughout the day and night, you will hear the names of the weather buoys and lighthouses from which data has been collected. You'll hear names like Sentry shoal, Pine Island, West Sea Otter Buoy, etc.

You must know where these reporting stations actually are for the weather to make sense. The easiest place to find this information is in your *Waggoner Cruising Guide*. All *Waggoner Guides* have a page titled "West Coast Marine Weather Observation Site." It lists:

- All marine weather reporting stations from Olympia to Ketchikan.

- All marine weather reporting radio stations and the areas they cover. For example WX1(WX = weather) covers Seattle, Cape Lazo, Alert Bay, and Klemtu.
- Marine weather reports are designed to give reports for the area you are in or around. For that reason, when you are near Klemtu and dial in to WX1, you'll hear the weather report for Klemtu and not the one for Seattle.
- When you listen to marine weather reports, they will often tell you phones numbers you can call to get the same weather report. Write these numbers down and have them on hand.

Collect Reported Information in a Dedicated Notebook

Collecting weather data is a bit of a job. The first few times you do it, you'll get things wrong, or you'll only get part of the information. It gets easier the more you do it. Really!

First, get yourself a spiral notebook or journal or white board to write on.

Next listen to the report. The first time through, try to collect the names of the buoys and lighthouses in the order they appear in the report.

Then listen to and jot down the synopsis, which will be given before the one-day and three-day forecasts.

Then listen to and jot down the information in the reports. You'll be very busy doing this because a weather buoy will provide:

- The name of the buoy.

- Wind speed in knots.
- Wave height, wave period (You want the wave period to be a greater number than the wave height).
- Air pressure and tendency. (Is the weather getting calmer, or not?)
- Air temperature.
- Water temperature.

Weather lighthouses provide:

- The station's name.
- Sky conditions (Clear, partly cloudy, cloudy, overcast, obscured).
- Visibility in miles.
- Weather elements (rain, rain shower, snow, drizzle, fog, thunder, and hail).
- Wind direction (direction from which the wind comes).
- Wind speed in knots (may include gust speed).
- Sea state (smooth, rippled, chop, moderate, or rough, and the wave height in feet).
- Swell height and direction (low = 0-2 meters, moderate = 2-4 meters, heavy = more than 4 meters).
- Remarks (may include dew point).

This is obviously a lot of information to jot down, so please create your own shortcuts or abbreviations for gathering this data. This gets easier with practice.

For example, I write only one or two letters of a weather station's name (i.e., O = West Sea Otter), and I write the highest predicted wind (i.e., 20 = 15-20 knots) instead of the range. Remember to note the wind direction because that will affect sea state (i.e. wind against current).

Note: Notice where the weather lighthouse provides swell height. When it says swell height is low at two meters, I want to advise you that two meters is six-and-a-half feet, which is not all that low for many cruising boats. It's best to listen to a buoy observation for actual wave height.

Decide If the Forecasted Conditions Will Provide You a Safe, Comfortable Passage

When deciding if the forecasted weather will help you have a safe, comfortable passage, it helps to know your planned route, including the direction of the currents during the time you plan to travel.

For example, if your plans include having the current push you in a favorable way, but you realize a twenty-knot wind will oppose that current (wind against current = standing waves), you might want to wait until a calmer day.

Or maybe you don't want to wait because you will be travelling through waters protected from the wind by mountains and trees.

It's your choice.

Sometimes you'll want to listen to the weather report throughout the day, especially if you're hearing of improving or worsening conditions.

For example, we were in Silva Bay holding off going across Georgia Strait to Pender Harbour, when we noticed that the Merry Island and Halibut Bank observation stations were reporting rapidly calming conditions. We decided to make the passage knowing that there would be about a half-hour of lump outside Silva Bay, but then we'd have a calm passage. And calm it was. Just like glass.

Also, don't assume that the forecast you heard just before you went to bed the night before will still be true when you wake up the next morning. It may, or it may not. Always listen to the weather before making a passage.

Short-Cruise Weather Gathering

For a short cruise of a week or two, you'll probably benefit from having Internet access on your smart phone and computer. You'll be able to access your already-downloaded apps for weather and sea state forecasts (PredictWind, SeaConditions, BuoyWeather, SailFlow, etc.).

You'll also probably spend most of your trip in more protected waters. A twenty-knot wind blowing in the Strait of Georgia will affect you less significantly if you're cruising in the protected waters of the Gulf Islands.

Still, the need to pay attention to the weather is vital. If a gale is forecasted, you'll want to be in a marina well fastened to the dock. If that's impossible, you'll want to be in an anchorage where you can let out enough anchor rode to keep you from dragging, especially toward a lee shore. In other words, the wind should blow you away from shore, rather than toward it.

Even if no gale is forecast, you'll want to know the wind's direction for anchoring. You'll want to avoid a situation where the wind blows directly into your anchorage. If an anchorage opens to the north, and a north wind is predicted, you can expect to be blown toward shore. Avoid situations like that.

Special Situations

The Pacific Northwest is known for its rain and fog. For cruisers, these conditions can be obstacles.

Rain impedes visibility. Some cruisers put Rain X on their windows to help the raid bead off. (Yes, Rain X now has a formula for plastic windows!) If you're boating in the rain, everyone should keep a lookout on the water. Logs and other debris are more difficult to see when it's raining. One nice thing about rain is that it cleans off your boat.

Fog also impedes visibility. Most boaters in the PNW wait for fog to lift before heading out in it. This is not so much because of other boats, but because of logs and deadheads that don't show up on the radar. If you don't have radar, I'd suggest you avoid making passages when there's a forecast for fog.

Chapter Twenty-One

Enjoying Your Cruise

Anchoring

Preferences ★ Cruising Guides ★ Depth ★ Weather Wakes
Bottom ★ Swinging ★ Stern Tie ★ Plan B
Weighing Anchor ★ Landing ★ Mooring Cans
Onboard Communication ★ Anchoring Basics
Snubbers and Bridles ★ Rafting

Anchoring in a Pacific-Northwest cove can be one of the most relaxing, visually appealing, and interesting experiences you have on your cruise. You get that feeling of being out in the wild, communing with nature, and marveling at all her strength, creativity, and beauty. Except if you've chosen the wrong anchorage for the weather forecast, or you haven't configured your anchor properly.

When anchoring, my priorities are to:

- Find a safe and comfortable, and hopefully beautiful, anchorage
- Find a safe and comfortable spot in the anchorage for us and our boat

- Feel secure.

It's easy to find a beautiful anchorage along the inside passage, but it's harder to find one that's safe and comfortable. Whether you're on a sailboat or powerboat, you'll want to follow the same procedure when looking for a good anchorage:

Preferences

First decide what you're looking for. Sometimes you'll just be spending the night and leaving the anchorage first thing in the morning. If so, you might not care so much about hiking and kayaking opportunities. Other times you may want to stay in an anchorage for a few days, and so you'll want to be in a place that offers a lot of protection from weather that comes from myriad directions, as well recreational prospects.

Cruising Guides

Then you'll look at your charts and read up on the area in the *Waggoner* Cruising Guide, *Northwest Boat Travel*, and other cruising guides, like the Dreamweaver Series. They will give you a plenty of information about the anchorage, its benefits and hazards, and recommendations about where and how to anchor there.

Depth

You're looking for depths of 10-30 feet. If the tide range is 20 feet, you'll want to opt for shallower water, but not too shallow. It all depends on whether your anchor rode is mostly heavy chain or if it's mostly rope. Through trial and error, learn how much rode you need in calm weather to stay put. If the wind pipes up, put out more rode. If you anchored at low tide, make sure you've added enough rode to keep you safe and grounded when the tide eventually reaches its maximum depth. The object is always to have your anchor set, and then to have enough rode lying flat on the ocean floor so that it settles into the sand and mud. That's what keeps you safe.

There are a few things you'll want to pay attention to regarding depths and tides:

- Canadian charts measure depth in metres. Their tide tables use both metres and feet. Be sure to check which is used in the table you're using.
- US charts measure depths in feet or fathoms (6 feet). Tide table generally measure depths in feet. Check to be sure.
- All charts tell you what datum is. Regarding tide changes, datum is the fixed starting depth for a measurement. For example, if the fixed starting depth is 30 feet, then a 2-foot rise in tide would mean the depth is 32 feet. Likewise a 2-foot drop in tide would mean the depth is 28'
- Datum for US tide tables uses Mean Lower Low Water and Mean Higher High Water. The MLLW is the average depth of the daily lower low for a span of many years. The MHHW is the average of daily highs over many years.
- Datum for Canadian tide table uses Higher High Water and Lower Low Water, rather than their average.
- In Canadian tide tables 1.6 metres means one and six-tenths of a meter. If a tide table says 1.6 feet, it

means one and six-tenths of a foot. In other words, 12 inches plus 7.2 inches (.6 x 12 inches = 7.2 inches).

Weather

You'll also want to listen to the weather so you know what to expect for the rest of the day or couple of days. If the wind is expected to reach higher than fifteen knots, you'll want to be in an anchorage that does not face directly into the oncoming wind. An anchorage that faces into the predicted wind could have uncomfortable wind waves and could expose you to being blown onto the lee shore if things turned nasty. We often look for anchorages where we see very few fallen trees; it's a sign the area is well protected from the wind.

Wakes

You'll want to be aware of ship, ferry, and other boat traffic just outside an anchorage. Even if the weather and wind are fair, heavy boat traffic outside an anchorage will create uncomfortable wakes inside the anchorage. Avoid these anchorages when possible.

Bottom

Sandy and muddy bottoms are usually good for holding. Rocky and very-grassy bottoms make it more difficult for anchors to catch hold and stay. *Waggoner, NW Boat Travel,* and the *Dreamweaver* series will advise on the holding qualities of the anchorages they describe.

Swinging

Your boat will swing on its anchor as the current flows in and then out of the anchorage. It will swing with the wind too. Your boat may swing faster than other boats, or it may swing slower, depending on its heft, its keel, and its living-space height.

When you anchor keep this in mind. If another boat that's already anchored requests you to move because it fears you may swing into it, unfortunately you should move.

If another boat anchors close enough to you that you feel uncomfortable, you may ask them to move.

Note: If all the boats in your immediate vicinity are swinging on one anchor, you endanger yourself and others if you put out two anchors or stern tie your boat. Likewise, if all the boats next to you are double anchored or stern tied, you should do the same, or move further away.

Stern-tie

In many anchorages along the Inside Passage, you may find the need to stern tie your boat. Maybe the anchorage is overcrowded. Or it's steep and deep. We try to avoid such anchorages, but sometimes it's unavoidable. To stern tie, you'd typically:

- Need 600' of polypropylene line on a spool situated on the stern of your boat, or facing the stern.
- Have your dinghy ready to deploy to shore.
- Anchor close to shore.
- Be dressed in clothing that offers protection when you reach shore like water shoes with skid-free bottoms and waterproof gloves.

- Have a length of sacrificial line to tie around a tree or rock.

After you've anchored, take your dinghy to shore along with your sacrificial line and the end of your propylene line, which spends out while you're traveling.

At the shore, loosely tie your sacrificial line around a sturdy, stationary tree.

Then thread the end of the propylene line through the loop and bring it all back into your dinghy.

Travel back to your boat and tie the end of the propylene line to your boat. Ta dah! You're stern tied.

To free yourself, untie the end of the propylene line from your boat and let it fall into the water. Drag the line back onto your boat, with the end piece arriving last. Spool the line as you retrieve it.

Boativated.com has a great description for doing this.

Plan B

Always have in mind an alternate anchorage or marina if the one you're in doesn't work out. Research it the same way you did for Plan A.

Weighing Anchor

When you depart from you anchorage, be prepared. You'll need:

- Water to wash mud off your anchor, chain, and/or rope.
- A knife to cut kelp from your anchor, chain, and/or rope.

Because muddy bottoms are terrific to anchor in, consider having a saltwater wash-down hose on your bow. This way you can wash off the anchor and rode before allowing them in your chain locker.

A second remedy for a muddy anchor and rode would be to have a long-lined tether tied to a bucket and to your boat. Drop the bucket into the sea water and retrieve it. You now have a way to wash down your chain, rope, and anchor.

Before you weigh anchor:

- Turn on your engine.
- Make the usual preparations you'd do if you were leaving a dock.
- Have one of you on the bow, and the other at the wheel.
- Have your chain locker prepared to receive the chain, rope, and anchor.
- Have predetermined hand signals that the person on the bow will give to the boat driver. These signals will ask the boat driver to move forward or backward slowly, to stop, or to veer to the left or right.

The actual weighing process is fairly straightforward. The chain or rope gets hauled aboard and stored in the chain locker in such a way that it is not tangled. Then the anchor is hauled up where it finds its home in the anchor roller on the bow, or it is tied to a stanchion.

The boat driver helps the anchor person by slowly driving toward the anchor until the anchor person signals that the boat should stop. The boat driver pays close attention to the anchor person's direction signals.

Sometimes the anchor is not where the boat driver assumes it should be.

Anchors usually come up easily. For those times when it doesn't, consider:

- Slowly twisting to the right, and then stopping to let things settle. Then twist to the left. Do several times.
- Slowly moving over the anchor and forward, and then stopping to let things settle. Do several times.

But ultimately best defense against having a snagged anchor is to avoid anchoring in spots where there has been logging operations, current or in the past, as well as places where there has been a landslide. Always check your charts and cruising references before dropping anchor.

Landing

One of the delights of anchoring is the potential for landing ashore by means of your dinghy, kayak, or paddle board. If you have pets on board, taking them ashore may be a necessity. If you plan to take your dinghy ashore, there are a few things you'll want to consider:

- If you land ashore during a rising tide, you'll need to have a very long bow line to tie to something higher than the tide will rise. Otherwise, you may come back to find that the only way to get to your dinghy is to swim to it.
- If you land ashore during an ebbing tide, you'll want to drop a stern anchor/bungee system [i.e. Anchor Buddy] before making your landing and tying up. Otherwise, you may come back to find

that you'll have to haul your dinghy a long way over land before getting it back in the water.

The reason you need to know the above is because in the Inside Passage the tide is always rising or falling.

Mooring Cans

Sometimes you can luck out and tie up to a mooring can if your boat length is less than 45'. Larger boats cannot use mooring cans because these boats need more swinging room than the can placement allows.

If you use a mooring can in the US or Canada, you will most likely be required to leave a payment. In Washington, you can purchase an annual pass for $5/foot to use marine park mooring buoys.

As for picking up a mooring can's line, some cruisers use a simple boat hook, while others swear by snagging the pick-up line at the boat's stern with a Happy Hooker or a Grab n Go, and walking it to the bow to cleat it off.

On *L'Esprit*, we really like our Johnson Grab n Go, but we prefer snagging the pick-up line at the bow so the lines connected to the buoy have no opportunity to tangle in our propellers. To do so, we use an extendable boat hook that's long enough to reach the pick-up line.

If your boat's bow climbs high out of the water, this may not work for you.

In any case, either hooker will have a long line, which you should cleat on to your boat before hooking the buoy.

Onboard Communication

When anchoring and snagging a mooring buoy's pick-up line, and when leaving, you'll want a clear method of communication between the person handling the anchor and the person driving the boat. I'd suggest you and the Captain develop hand signals which the person on the bow will use to communicate to the driver.

At a minimum, these signals will communicate:

- The direction the boat should move.
- How fast the boat should move.
- Whether the boat should be stopped or moving.

If you find you need additional signals than these, please address your needs.

Another valuable communicating device is a wireless, hands-free walkie-talkie headset device, such as a pair of Eartec 2 Simultalk Cyber Headsets.

Anchoring Basics

When you've found the right spot in your anchorage:

- Face your boat into the wind or into current if there is no wind.
- Stop your boat and wait for it to begin going backward slightly. If it doesn't naturally do this, bump your boat in reverse for a second or two.
- Drop your anchor while keeping your boat going in a very slow, backward direction. Do not, however, keep the boat in gear. If you need to, just bump it backward a bit at a time. Keeping the boat in gear may cause the anchor to drag.
- Stop letting the rode out when you have the proper amount out.

Snubbers and Bridles

After your anchor is satisfactorily set, you'll want to add a snubber or bridle, which acts as shock absorber that takes tension off your anchor windlass. (If you value your windlass, you will do this!)

Use a snubber when forecasted conditions are mild; use a bridle when conditions are forecasted to be windier and therefore wavier.

You can make snubbers and bridles, or you can buy them. Make sure your bridle's:

- Line has a diameter wide enough for your boat's length and weight.
- Line stretches well.
- Chain grabber fits your chain. When you first start using your bridle, pay attention to it when in windy conditions. We had issues with our chain grabber dislodging. You may need to reinforce the hold using a wire tie.

Rafting

Rafting is when you let another boat tie up to you, and they use you as their anchor. It is a common practice in the Inside Passage, especially among boaters who are travelling together.

If you expect to be in a situation where you'll be rafting, take these issues into consideration:

- If you are the biggest boat of the group, you will probably, but not always, be asked to be the anchor boat. It is a good idea for the biggest or heaviest boat to be the anchor.
- Know where your generator and heater vents are, if you have them. These vents can express hot air

or fumes that could damage another boat and its occupants. Carbon monoxide is a silent killer.
- If you're in a cove or bay to which you may be exposed to an incoming storm, consider not rafting.
- Likewise with coves and bays exposed to wakes, which can make rafting quite uncomfortable, even dangerous.
- Consider adding a stern-tie. This will make it impossible for your boats to swing, which may be exactly what you want if space is limited. You can have one stern-tie, or both boats can stern tie.
- It is not unheard of to raft three, four, or five boats together. In well-protected coves, this can be a good idea, not to mention fun.
- Be aware of the other boat's rigging that may get confused in your own, and plan accordingly. In other words, if you are two sailboats, you'll want your masts and rigging not exactly next to each other.

Before rafting, whether you'll be rafting to another boat or they to you, have the following conditions met:

- You have decided beforehand to which side of each boat the rating will take place. Always raft so your bows face the same direction.
- Decide beforehand who is going to do what. For example, if you are the tied-to or host boat, you'll all be needed on deck to take the lines of the tying-to or guest boat. If you're the guest boat, one of you will be driving while the other will be handing the bow, stern, and mid-ship lines that

will be given to the host boat when positioned next to it. On *L'Esprit* we commonly tie the mid-ship before the bow and stern. We try to tie the bow last because we want our sterns snug so our swim steps are close so we can step onto each other's boat more easily. If your boats don't have swim steps, this is not an issue.

Use plenty of fenders. Consider putting an extra fender or two between the bow and mid-ship. You'll thank yourself, because rafting is not always a graceful event.

Consider having one fender available on an as-needed basis. On *L'Esprit*, we call this our roving fender. If we suddenly need a temporary fender during the raft-up phase, we simply dangle it over the side until the emergency has passed.

Set your fenders to the right level to both protect your boat and theirs.

Doubly secure your fender lines with a clove hitch followed by a half hitch. You don't want one of your fenders to become accidentally untied.

If you are the host boat, you do not have to have your lines ready. Instead, make sure there is a bow, mid-ship, and stern cleat available for the tying-to boat to cleat to.

If you are the guest boat, have a bow, mid-ship, and stern dock line ready to give to the host boat. Make sure these three lines are first secured to your boat.

When planning to approach the host boat, the guest boat should take into consideration the wind and current. The guest boat should also know that it may take more than one try to accomplish the raft up.

The actual act of rafting goes like this:

- The host boat anchors in a suitable spot where there is room for two or more boats and has a good-holding bottom. This may take a while, so the guest boat(s) should be patient while the host boat is satisfying its need to be securely anchored and has its gotten its snubber or bridle on, as well as its stern line if using one.
- Once done, the host boat Captain and First-Mate go on deck to receive lines and to protect their boat from accidental lurches.
- The guest boat, after its lines and fenders are prepared, slowly positions itself to raft up. The driver is driving slowly, but regularly adding momentum when needed (bumping the engine), and the line-handler is holding the first line intended to be tied.
- When a line from the guest boat comes to the host boat, it can either be tied off on the host boat, or looped around a cleat and pulled back onto the guest boat. The latter makes it possible for the guest boat to easily slip away if it needs to leave.
- For the final alignment, make sure people on the guest and host boat can step onto each others' boats. Check that all lines are secure.

When leaving a raft-up, the guest boat starts its engines before untying and gathering its lines from the host boat. When untied, slowly drive away. The host boat crew should ideally be onboard to watch and assist this process.

Chapter Twenty-Two

Enjoying Your Cruise

Docking

Plan Ahead ★ Know Where You're Going
Happy Landing ★ Sweet Goodbyes
Safety Check ★ Rafting

Docking and undocking a boat, like an airplane's take-off and landing, can be an intense exercise in judgment. The more you do it, the better you'll become.

As First Mate, you and the Captain will need to decide on who takes on what responsibilities. One of you will be the boat driver and one of you will be the one who brings the lines from the boat to the dock and cleats them off.

When docking and undocking a boat, my primary motivations are:

- To land at a dock and to leave it safely and securely.
- To feel and be safe during the whole procedure.
- To land the boat safely and securely.

Boaters all have an archive of frightening and hilarious docking stories. Maybe they tried to leave the dock with a line still attached to the cleat. Or they threw their line to someone on the dock who had no idea what to do with it. The best way to avoid having too many horrid or hilarious docking stories is to:

- Plan ahead.
- Prepare for as many contingencies as you can think of.
- Have plenty of fenders.
- Drive slowly, but use short bursts of speed when needed.
- Step onto the dock, rather than leaping to it.

Plan Ahead

Before ever leaving the dock, read and view websites and YouTube videos explain how to dock boats similar to yours. The website for this book has some useful links.

While reading up on docking and undocking, know that docking a sailboat differs from docking a powerboat. Likewise docking a boat with thrusters differs from docking a boat without them. And docking a dual-engine boat differs from docking a single engine boat. Focus your learning on the type of boat you have.

If you plan to step to the dock from your boat's stern, consider asking for a slip a couple of feet longer than your boat. I suggest this because if the slip is the exact length of you boat, you will have to wait until your boat is all the way in the slip before being able to get off. If you try to get off when the boat is not yet all the way in, you have nowhere to step but into the water. I learned this lesson the hard way.

Before entering the marina, idle outside a bit to get yourselves organized.

Make sure your fenders are placed vertically to provide the most protection from the dock and other boats. In other words, if you are sharing a dock with another boat, you'll want the fenders for the dock side to be one length, but the fenders for the other side another length.

Be prepared to make quick fender-length changes. Practice tying clove hitches so you can do them with your eyes closed. The same can be said for bowline knots and other knots you'll frequently need in emergencies.

Make sure all dock lines have one end cleated to your boat's deck. Then flake the lines so you or others on the dock can grab the lines from the boat without aid. Make sure the lines are OUTSIDE all the rails and stanchions, otherwise you'll be in a fine mess.

On *L'Esprit*, we added a cam cleat to the stern of the boat so a mid-line strung from mid-ships can be easily accessible from the stern upon landing.

Know Where You're Going

Your boat's driver should know exactly to what dock your boat is headed.

If you are visiting a marina, look at a chart of the marina in *Waggoner, NW Boat Travel, The Burgee*, your navigation software, or Active Captain. If there is any confusion, call the dock master. Don't enter until you are clear where you are going.

Your boat's driver should know in which direction the current is flowing and the wind is blowing.

Happy Landing

Slowly drive the boat into the slip or next to the dock. If the wind is head-on and blowing you against you, give the boat some more power if it seems safe.

For landing purposes, you might consider having any of the following on board:

- Landing Loop Docking Pole
- Floating, non-telescoping boat hook
- The Boat Loop
- Grapnel anchor tied to a long line.

The Landing Loop and Boat Loop can be used on dock cleats, but not bull rails. A boat hook can be used on cleats and some bull rails. A grapnel anchor can be used for bull rails, provided you're, say, three feet of the dock; you don't want to miss your target and have the anchor come back and hit your boat or get caught in the props.

The person going to the dock should not do so without wearing a floatation device and solid, non-slip shoes.

The person going to the dock should step from the boat to the dock, rather than leaping. Besides the fact that PNW is quite cold, one can be crushed between the boat and the dock. Better to back out and start over than to chance harm to one of you.

Docking a sailboat differs from docking a powerboat

On a sailboat, the person stepping to the dock usually does so off the widest part of the boat, near mid-ships. Because a sailboat's deck is generally lower than a powerboat's, stepping from the deck to the dock is easier. This person holds the loose end of the mid-ship mooring line when stepping onto the dock and then immediately takes a wrap around the nearest cleat or bull rail. Then the person goes for the stern line to wrap around another cleat or bull rail. The boat is then stable. If the boat needs to be brought forward or backward, that can be done when the engine is off and two people are on the dock.

On a powerboat, the person stepping to the dock usually does so off the swim step or off a side near the rear. If the person steps off the swim step, the loose end of the stern line should be taken to the dock and tied off quickly before grabbing the mid-ship line and tying it off on another cleat or bull rail.

If the person steps off near mid-ship, either the loose end of the stern line or the mid-ship line is taken to shore and made fast around a cleat or bull rail. In either case, the bow line is tied last. And in either case, the boat can be repositioned when the engine is off and two people are on shore.

If the driver backs into the slip, the same general rules apply:

- Tie off the mid-ship and stern mooring lines first, in whatever order works best.
- Turn off the engine before repositioning and finalizing the dock lines.

If someone is on the dock to help you land, make it a priority to give them the mid-ship line first. It is not recommended to give anyone your bow line because their instinct is to tie it off, which will push your stern out. If you do find yourself in a situation where you must give them the bow line, tell them to keep it very loose.

Consider having chafe guards for your mooring lines, especially when the docks are rough bull rails, which can really eat through lines in a blow. I actually hate the look of ours, but I'll never give them up because of the extra protection they provide.

Cleats and bull rails

Throughout the Inside Passage you'll be tying up to dock cleats and dock bull rails.

Cleats are usually metal and look like anvils bolted to the dock. If you do a web search for "How to tie up to a dock cleat," you'll find lots of illustrations for how to do this. Study these guides and then practice, practice, practice until the movements take hold in your muscle memory.

Whatever you do, always start your first wrap on a cleat by moving the line UNDER either the left or right shoulder. Then you basically continue with horizontal over-under-over-under movements until you finish off your wrap. I could describe what making your final wrap looks like, but I'd suggest you actually watch the movements on a YouTube video.

In Canada and Alaska you'll see more bull rails on docks than cleats. Again, search the Internet for illustrations for how to do this. CaptnMike.com has a lot of good information about tying to bull rails.

Bull rails are sturdy wooden or metal beams bolted to the dock via risers. The risers are maybe half a foot high, so there's space between the dock and the beam for your dock line to pass through. The object is to wrap your line vertically around the beam once or twice and tie it off.

The big question is: Should the wrap be over-then-under, or the opposite, under-than-over?

Unlike the pattern for dock cleats, I don't think it matters initially whether you start your wrap from the top or the bottom. For me, it's always easier to start from the top. Others may feel the opposite. I say do what feels comfortable in the initial docking process.

But then things change.

After you're docked safely and soundly, I strongly suggest that you make sure your bull-rail wrap starts from the bottom and then wraps over the top and tied.

Here's why.

The outside surfaces of bull rails are often quite rough and splintered. These splinters can snag dock lines, which can cause a myriad of problems when you're departing the dock.

When your dock line starts its wrap from the bottom, it makes it possible for the line to be untied and simply laid on the dock. From here, the line can be pulled back onto the boat with little danger of snagging.

If you'll be cruising in areas rife with bull rails, consider using chafe guards on your dock lines. I know people who have lost good dock lines because a bull rail's roughness chafed through their line in a big blow. As I've said earlier, I hate the look of our chafe guards, but I love how they protect our lines.

Leaving the Dock

When leaving a dock, be prepared. Unplug the electricity. Turn on your engine. Inspect your electrical panel to make sure you have the correct circuits on. Have your helm station ready to go. Check for obstacles and traffic.

If someone is on the dock to help you untie your lines, you're in luck. Usually the bow is untied first, then the stern or mid-ship, depending on your boat.

If no one is on the dock to help you untie your lines, you and the Captain will need to help each other. What I've found to be quite helpful is to have me standing mid-ship holding the mid-ship line, which is single-looped around a cleat or from UNDER a bull rail. Capt. Dave then unties the other lines and boards our boat. When he puts the boat in reverse, I unloop the mid-ship line from the cleat, or I throw the bull-railed line onto the dock and quickly retrieve it. I've found if I try to do this with the line looped over the bull rail, it has a tendency to snag, with dangerous results.

Safety Check

Again, the person going to the dock should not do so without wearing a floatation device and solid, non-slip shoes.

Also again, the person going to the dock should step from the boat to the dock, rather than leaping. Besides the fact that PNW is quite cold, one can be crushed between the boat and the dock. Better to back out and start over than to chance harm to one of you.

Communication is vital. Consider using a pair of Eartec 2 Simultalk Cyber Headsets while docking. If you do, please try to provide each other only the necessary information such as:

- Distance from dock
- Obstructions
- Status (i.e., you're on the dock, you have the stern tied off, etc.)

After docking, debrief. What went well? What were the problems and their possible solutions? Learning to dock a boat well takes practice. Blaming one another for problems solves little.

We always operate from the assumption that we are really doing our best. Some things take longer to master than others.

What you're after is refining your abilities and having easier, safe entrances and departures. It will come. The more practice you have, the better you'll become. Honest!

Rafting at the Dock

As with anchoring, don't be surprised if you need to raft up to another boat in a marina. When space is limited, this is often requested of you. In fact, don't be surprised if a workboat simply ties to you without first requesting to do so. Ultimately, mariners help mariners, especially working mariners.

If you are asked to be the host boat:

- Put out plenty of securely-tied fenders.
- Have the raft-side cleats freed up.
- Help the guest boat tie up to you.

If you are the guest boat:

- Ask the host boat if you can raft up. Sometimes a marina will require this of a host boat.
- Secure your docking lines to your boat.
- Slowly, come astride the host boat. If they come out to help you, you're in luck. Hand them your lines to make fast on their cleats. If they are not aboard, one of you will need to reach over and secure your midline to their mid-ship cleat. Once that is done, and you are semi-secure, get your bow and stern lines to the other boat, get on their boat, and make t hem secure.
- When leaving, start your engines before untying your lines. Move away slowly, using your boat hook as necessary.

Chapter Twenty-Three

Enjoying Your Cruise

Fair Winds!

I wish you many happy days as you cruise the Pacific Northwest's Inside Passage.

If you learn new ideas that you'd like to share on the FirstMatesGuide.com, please send me your information. I can't wait to hear from you.

Also if you think you have some solutions not yet considered, please share that too. Again, I can't wait to hear from you.

And one last thing: Have some boat cards made up before your trip so you can give them to all the new friends you'll make during your cruise. It still fascinates me how strong the ties develop between the *L'Esprit* crew and the crews we meet along the way. It is truly one of the unexpected delights of the cruising the waters from Olympia and Glacier Bay.

After Matter

Appendix

Cruising Terminology, p. 281
Main Marine-Radio Channels, p. 286
Horn Blasts, p. 288
Marine-Radio Lingo, p.289
Marine-Radio Scripts, p. 290

Cruising Terminology

The following is a list of generic terms you may hear while boating. I've purposely not included words specific to only sailboats or powerboats. These are words you'll hear during on marine-radio conversations and when talking with fellow cruisers at docks and at anchor. If you'd like a more complete list, look at Wikipedia's "Glossary of Nautical Terms," or visit the website NauticEd.org/SailingTerms.

- ABAFT, AFT – toward the back or stern of a vessel
- APPARENT WIND – the direction from which the wind appears to be coming while your boat is travelling through the water. True wind is the actual direction from which the wind is coming, if you were standing on land.
- ATHWARTSHIP – something positioned from one side of the boat to the other and perpendicular to the keel.
- AWEIGHT – to lift the anchor in preparation to sail.
- BEAM SEA – when waves break along side of your boat, rather than the bow or stern.
- BEARING – the imaginary line between one point and another.
- BIGHT – either an indentation along the coastline, or a loop in the middle of a line.
- BILGE – area in the hull's bottom where liquids (water, etc.) collect and can be pumped out.
- BOW – the front of the boat.

- BROACH – when a boat makes a sudden turn because of having lost control because of being overpowered by a wave or by the wind.
- BUOY – a floating navigational aid or mooring apparatus.
- CHART – a navigation map. Maps are for land use, charts are for marine use.
- CHOCK – an opening at the top of the hull through which dock lines can be guided.
- COCKPIT, FLYBRIDGE – seating area where running controls are located.
- DECK – a boat's horizontal walking surface, usually attached to the top of the hull.
- DISPLACEMENT – the weight of the water that is displaced when the boat is in the water.
- DRAFT, DRAUGHT – a boat's depth from the waterline to the boat's lowest point.
- EYE SPLICE – a closed loop at the end of a line whose strength is highly valued.
- FAIR – smooth or helpful.
- FATHOM – 6 feet or 1.8 meters
- FETCH – the distance across which the wind and waves have traveled.
- FLOTSAM, JETSAM, LAGAN – All are debris. Flotsam is floating wreckage. Jetsam is debris thrown overboard. Lagan is wreckage or debris on the sea bottom.
- FLUKE – the anchor parts that dig into the sand and mud.
- FOREPEAK – below-deck area at the bow of the boat.
- FOUNDER – to fill with water and sink.

- GALLEY – the kitchen.
- GUNWALE – the hull's top edge.
- HARBOR MASTER – the person responsible for operating the marina.
- HEAD – the bathroom, and more specifically the toilet.
- HULL – the shell of a floating vessel; the part that touches the water.
- HULL SPEED – the fastest speed any specific hull can travel through the water. Note: Planing hulls rise above the water rather than through it.
- JETTY – a man-made breakwater or sea wall.
- KNOT – refers to speed per hour. 1 nautical mile equals 1.85 kilometers or 1.15 miles per hour.
- LANYARD – a rope for tying one thing to something else.
- LAZARETTE – a deck compartment for stowing gear.
- LEE, ALEE – facing away from the wind.
- ALOFT – overhead.
- LEG – a step of a voyage; the distance and time from one destination to the next.
- LIST – when a vessel leans because of its own unbalanced weight.
- MAGNETIC NORTH – the direction to the North Magnetic Pole. True north is the direction to the geographical North Pole.
- MAKE FAST – tie down.
- MANIFEST – list of passengers for customs.
- MARLINSPIKE – a rope-working tool for making eye splices, etc.

- MIDSHIPS, AMIDSHIP, ABREAST – the boat's middle section.
- MOOR – to dock or tie off a boat.
- OVERFALLS – steep, breaking seas that come from wind against current and strong currents in shallows.
- PEAK – see Forepeak.
- PORT – the left side.
- PORT TACK – when the wind blows from the port side of the boat. Port tack sailboats have to give way to starboard tack boats, whose wind blows from the starboard side of their boats.
- REEFER – the refrigerator.
- SCREW – a propeller.
- SKEG – a propeller protector that protrudes from the keel.
- SKIFF – a small boat.
- SLIP – a dock between wharves.
- SPLICE – to join ropes by unraveling them and then intertwining them back together.
- STANCHION – vertical poles on the deck that support life lines.
- TAND-ON-VESSEL – the boat maintaining its course and speed in a collision-prevention situation. The other boat changes course or speed.
- STARBOARD – the right side.
- STERN, ASTERN – the back of the boat.
- TENDER – in yachting it's your dinghy.
- TRAFFIC SEPARATION SCHEME – the lanes specified for ship traffic.
- TRANSOM – the back was of a boat's stern.

- TRUE WIND - the direction from which the wind is actually coming. It differs from apparent wind, which is the direction from which the wind appears to be coming while your boat is travelling through the water.
- V-BERTH – the forward cabin, named for its usual shape.
- WATERLINE – the usual level where the water rises to on a boat's hull.
- WEIGH – lift.
- WIDE BERTH – plenty of room.
- WINDLASS – a horizontal winch, usually used to pull up an anchor.
- WINDWARD – facing the wind.

Main Marine Radio Channels

Washington VHF Channels

05A – Vessel Traffic Service Seattle – Northern Puget Sound
06 – Intership Safety
09 – Intership and Ship-shore all Vessels and Calling and Reply for Pleasure Vessels
13 – Vessel Bridge to Vessel Bridge – Large Vessels
14 – Vessel Traffic Service – So. Puget Sound
16 – International Distress, Safety, & Calling
22 – Coast Guard Liaison (to talk w/CG)
66A- Port Operations- (usually marinas)
67 – Intership for all vessels (US only)
68 – Intership and ship-shore, non-commercial
69 - Intership and ship-shore, non-commercial
72 – Intership only for all vessels (US only)
78 - Intership and ship-shore, non-commercial

British Columbia VHF Channels

05A – Vessel Traffic Service Seattle – Strait of Juan de Fuca west of Victoria
06-Intership Safety
09- Intership and ship-shore all vessels
11 – Vessel Traffic Service – North and east of Victoria
12- Vessel Traffic Service – Vancouver and Howe Sound
16- International Distress, Safety & Calling
66A- Port operations – usually marinas
67- Intership and ship-shore
68- Intership and ship-shore, non-commercial
69- Intership and ship-shore, non-commercial

71 – Vessel Traffic Service – Northern Strait of Georgia to Cape Caution

72 – Intership

73 – Intership and ship-shore

74 – Vessel Traffic Service Victoria – Victoria-Fraser River

83 – Coast Guard Liaison (talk w/CG)

For a complete list of all marine radio frequencies and their uses, go on Wikipedia and enter: Marine VHF Radio. When you scroll down, you'll find what you need. You can find a complete list of US frequencies by Googling Navigation Center Maritime Telecommunications. Also, find these channels in this book's appendices.

What the Horn Blasts Mean

Horn blasts aren't used a lot by cruisers, but they are important to understand. Even if you never blast your horn, ships and tugs around you definitely will. You'll want to know what their horn signal means so you can respond if necessary.

1 short blast means the ship wants to pass the other boat down ship's port side.

2 short blasts mean the ship wants to pass the other boat down the ship's starboard side.

3 short blasts tell everyone the ship is backing up.

5 short blasts mean danger because the ship doesn't understand the other boat's intentions and wants to make sure everyone will be safe.

1 long blast means the ship is entering or leaving a blind turn, or it's near an obstructed area, or it's leaving its dock or anchorage.

1 long blast every two minutes is the ship's fog horn which it uses when there's low visibility.

Marine-Radio Lingo

When calling large vessels, vessel traffic, as well as many fishing and recreational boats, you may hear marine radio lingo, as you read in the above conversation. "Copy that" and "Roger that" are examples of such lingo. Here's a list of phrases you'll commonly hear and will probably pick up yourself the more you cruise:

ROGER, ROGER THAT, COPY, COPY THAT – means you understand. It doesn't necessarily mean you agree or will comply, however.

WILCO –means you will comply. Don't use WILCO with either ROGER or COPY.

OVER – means you're done with your thought, but not the conversation.

OUT – means you're done with the whole conversation.

AFFIRMATIVE – means yes.

NEGATIVE – means no.

NINER – means nine and not to be confused with five.

SAY AGAIN, SAY AGAIN YOUR LAST – means please repeat

STAND BY – means wait a minute

READY TO COPY – means ready to write something down

BREAK – means you're starting a new thought

Marine-Radio Scripts

Mayday Call (dire emergency):

MAYDAY MAYDAY MAYDAY This is SAIL/POWER vessel YOUR BOAT'S NAME. We are approximately LOCATION. We are SITUATION. We are a LENGTH, BRAND OR STYLE, COLOR. Request immediate assistance. OVER.

Pon Pon Call (imminent emergency):

PON PON, PON PON, PON PON. This is SAIL/POWER vessel YOUR BOAT'S NAME. We are approximately LOCATION. We are SITUATION. We are a LENGTH, BRAND OR STYLE, COLOR. We have NUMBER OF PEOPLE on board. Request immediate assistance. OVER

Securite Call (reporting danger):

SECURITE SECURITE SECURITE This is SAIL/POWER vessel YOUR BOAT'S NAME AND LENGTH. We are at LOCATION. We are STATE SITUATION. All concerned traffic call your boat's nameon Ch. 16. OVER.

Calling a Marina - example:

YOU: Friday Harbor Marina, Friday Harbor Marina, Friday Harbor Marina. This is the motor vessel My Boat, My Boat, My Boat. Over.

FH MARINA: My Boat, this is Friday Harbor Marina. OVER

YOU: Friday Harbor Marina, we are a 45-foot power boat looking for moorage tonight and tomorrow night. We would like a starboard tie and thirty amps of power. OVER.

FH MARINA: We have a spot for you. How far out are you? OVER

YOU: Approximately 2 miles. OVER

FH MARINA: Please call us when you are at the harbor entrance and we will give you your slip assignment. OVER.

YOU: Thank you, Friday Harbor Marina. We will call when we reach the harbor entrance. My Boat monitoring 66A. OUT.

FH MARINA: Friday Harbor monitoring 66A. OUT.

Calling a Ship- example:

YOU: This is My Boat, My Boat, My Boat, calling the black-hulled freighter just off Turn Point, calling the black-hulled freighter just off Turn Point, calling the black-hulled freighter just off Turn Point. OVER.

SHIP: This is the freighter Endless Seas. OVER. (if you've called them on Ch. 16, they'll probably ask you to switch to Ch. 13.)

YPI: Endless Seas, we are the white powerboat approximately 2 nautical miles off your starboard bow. Our intention is to avoid you. What are your intentions? OVER

SHIP: Roger that. We plan to make a 20 degree turn to our port in 3 minutes. OVER

YOU: Copy that (or Roger that). Thank you, Captain, we will steer to our port to avoid you. OVER.

SHIP: Thank you. Endless Seas OUT.

Calling Vessel Traffic — example:

YOU: Victoria Vessel Traffic, Victoria Vessel Traffic, Victoria Vessel Traffic. This is My Boat, My Boat, My Boat. OVER.

VVT: My Boat, this is Victoria Vessel Traffic. OVER.

YOU: Traffic, My Boat. We will be crossing northbound from Port Townsend to Cadboro Bay. We request a traffic update. OVER.

VVT: Copy that, My Boat. The tanker Golden Ore is eastbound in Juan de Fuca Strait and the passenger vessel Alaska Pride is southbound nearing Beaumont Shoal. OVER

YPI: Copy that, Traffic. Thank you. My Boat back to 16. OUT.

VVT: Victoria Traffic OUT.

Calling the Coast Guard - example:

YOU: Canadian Coast Guard, Canadian Coast Guard, Canadian Coast Guard. This is My Boat, My Boat, My Boat. OVER.

CCG: My Boat, this is the Canadian Coast Guard. Are you in any danger? OVER

YOU: No (or negative). OVER

CCG: Switch to 83. OVER.

YOU: Switching to 83. OVER. (at the point, switch to 83, and call the Coast Guard again).

YOU: Canadian Coast Guard, this is My Boat on Channel 83. OVER.

CCG: This is Canadian Coast Guard. OVER.

YOU: Canadian Coast Guard, I'd like to report a large deadhead floating outside the entry to Pender Harbour. OVER.

CCG: Copy. What is its approximate latitude and longitude? OVER

YOU: (speaking slowly) 49 04 31 north, 12 21 55 west. OVER

CCG: Copy. We will broadcast that for mariners in the vicinity. OVER.

YOU: Copy. My Boat back to 16. OUT.

CCG: Canadian Coast Guard monitoring 16. OUT.

Calling Another Vessel – example:

YOU: Seabolt, Seabolt, Seabolt. This is My Boat, My Boat, My Boat. OVER

THEM: Seabolt here. OVER.

YOU: Switch to 72. OVER

THEM: Copy. Switching to 72. OVER. (You both switch to 72)

YOU (or them): Seabolt. This is My Boat. OVER.

THEM: Hey, how the heck are you? OVER

YOU: Great! (Your conversation can be very natural now, because you are no longer on the emergency or ship channels.) OVER

YOU at end of conversation: My Boat back to 16. OUT.

THEM: Seabolt back to 16. OUT

About the Author

For the last twenty-five-years, Joanne Rodasta Wilshin has cruised the off-shore waters of Southern California; the bays of Baja and the Chesapeake; and, of late, the Pacific Northwest's Inside Passage. Every area described in this book she has visited with her husband Dave Wilshin, aboard their power vessel *L'Esprit*.

She and Dave moved to Washington in 2010 and sold their Mason sailboat *Always* and purchased *L'Esprit*. Then began their journey to learn the ropes of boating on the beautiful waters from Olympia to Glacier Bay, which they found so different from their previous cruising grounds.

Never having been one to leave all the "boat stuff" to the Captain, Joanne worked to understand the waters, the weather, the fine points of driving a power boat and navigating, as well as the art of provisioning for two- or three-month cruises. To her, striving to be a good First-Mate is the first step to having a safe and fun cruise.

She's grateful for the knowledge she has gleaned from her fellow members of the Fidalgo Yacht Club as well as the many NW cruisers she's met while cruising.

Visit her website FirstMatesGuide.com. to find links for most everything in this book, plus more.

Joanne lives in Anacortes, WA, with her husband Dave.

Index

A

Anacortes, *3, 4, 7, 16, 30, 41, 42, 43, 181, 183, 295*
Anchor lights, *88*
Anchoring, *10, 15, 27, 63, 170, 208, 254, 263*
    Communication, during, *262*
    Depth, *255*
    Landing dinghy, *261*
    Rafting, *264*
    Snubbers, bridles, *264*
    Stern tie, *258*
    Weather, *257*
    Weighing anchor, *259*
Anchoring Basics
    Basics of, *263*

B

Backfire-Flame Arrestor, *76, 82*
Bellingham, *41, 42, 43*
Bells, *76, 82*
Bills, paying on time, *161*
Binoculars, *117*
Boat Cards, *166*
Boat Library, *9, 14, 90*
    Boat Repairs, *90, 94*
    Finding Harbors and Anchorages, *93*
    Safe Navigation, *91*
    Staying Healthy, *94*
Boat Notebook, *9, 14, 15, 19, 21, 59, 60, 61, 66, 67, 68, 69, 72, 73, 74, 79, 84, 86, 89, 94, 107, 108, 121, 123, 126, 134, 155, 158, 159, 166, 167, 171, 178, 180, 187, 188, 193, 206, 244*
Boatowner's Mechanical and Electrical Manual, *31, 36, 69, 94, 178*
Broughtons. the, *33, 35, 37, 51, 53, 54, 66, 91, 93, 104, 105, 185, 190, 191, 209, 211, 237, 248*

C

Calder, Nigel, *31*
Cape Caution, rounding, *239*
Cash, getting, *165*
Chartering or Owning, *29*
City, cruising in, *242*
Comfort Foods, *98, 99, 100*
Credit-card safety, *162*
Cruising Areas, *37*
    Broughtons, *51*

295

Desolation Sound, *49*
Discovery Islands and Passage, *49*
Gulf Islands, *43*
Johnstone Strait, *51*
North Puget Sound, *40*
Northern Georgia Strait, *47*
Noth Coast of BC, *54*
Queen Charlotte Strait, *51*
San Juan Islands, *41*
SE Alaska, *56*
South Puget Sound, *38*
Sunshine Coast, *45*
Vancouver, city of, *45*
Cruising Tasks, *59, 61*
Current
    Direction, *200*
    Slack, *201*
Currents, *197*
    Current information, *198*
    Estimating speed, *207*
    Line graphs, *203*
    Maximum velocities, *205*
    Moon Phase, *206*
    Tables, *202*
    Wind against current, *208*
Customs, *179*
    Alaska to Canada. *See* Canada to Alaska
    Canada from Washington, *183*
    Clearance number, *187*
    Courtesy flags, *188*
    Declaring items, *184*
    Getting ready for, *180*
    Nexus, CanPass, *184*
    US from Canada, 183

D

Desolation Sound, *33, 36, 37, 40, 49, 50, 91, 92, 93, 104, 106, 181, 190, 191, 209, 212*
Dinghy, *64, 120, 167, 170, 177*
Discovery Islands, *33, 37, 49, 50, 91, 93, 209*
Discovery Passage, *49*
Dixon Entrance, *241*
Docking, *10, 15, 27, 63, 268, 271*
    Aids to landing, *271*
    Bull rails, *273*
    Cleats, *273*
    Leaving, *274*
    Rafting at the dock, *276*
Dreamspeaker Series, *42, 44, 46, 50, 53, 91, 93, 215*
Driving boat, exercise, *224*

E

EPIRB, *69, 134*
EPIRBS. *See* Epirb

F

Fidalgo Yacht Club, *16*
Fire Extinguisher, *81*
Fire Extinguishers, *76*
First Mate, *16*
First-aid kit, *115*
Fishing boats, *232*
Float Plan, *189*
Float planes, *231*
Floatation Jackets and Vests, *76, 77*
Following seas

Wave period, *237*
Following Seas, *237*

G

Garbage, *96, 97*
Georgia Strait, *33, 37, 47, 163,*
　191, 211, 238, 239, 248, 251
　Crossing, *238*
Gulf Islands, *30, 33, 37, 43, 44, 45,*
　92, 93, 181, 209, 252

H

Horn blasts, meaning, *87*

I

Insurance, *156*
　Boat, *157*
　Health, *158*
　Home and car, *157*
　Salvage Right, *123*
Internet, *150*
Internet Apps, *151*

J

Johnstone Strait, *50, 51, 238*

L

L'Esprit., *20, 122*
Lagoons, *196, 212*
Life Rings, *76, 78*
life sling, *78*
Lights, meaning of, *88*

Local vs. Long Distance Cruising.
　See Long Distance Cruising
Locks, *225*

M

Mail, *164*
Man-overboard, *27, 118*
Marine-Radio Scripts, *127, 132,*
　279, 289
Medicine, *94, 115*
Mooring Cans, *262*

N

Navigating, *10, 15, 68, 90, 151,*
　214
Navigation Aids, *224*
North Coast of BC, *54*
North Puget Sound, *40*
Northwest Boat Travel, *32, 35, 36,*
　37, 39, 41, 42, 44, 46, 48, 50,
　53, 55, 57, 91, 242, 243, 255

P

Ports and Passes, *39, 41, 43, 45,*
　46, 48, 50, 53, 55, 91, 198, 212
Provisioning, *9, 14, 27, 28, 33, 55,*
　66, 96, 100
　comfort foods, *100*
　Foods that store well, *101*
　Galley Notebook, *107*
　Gathering and preparing food,
　　108
　Ingredients, *102*
　Map or diagram for
　　provisioning, *111*

297

Recipes and ideas, 101
Storage plan, *110*
Tools for the galley, *105*

Q

Queen Charlotte Strait, *51*, *237*, *240*, *248*

R

Radio, marine channels, *127*, *128*, *285*
Radio, ship to ship, *86*
Rapids and Narrows, *209*, *234*
    Rivers meet the Sea, *211*
Route creating, *215*
Route, following, *217*
Rules of the Road, *218*
    Pecking order, *218*
    Right of way for sailboats, *221*
Running lights, *87*

S

Sail or Power, *27*
San Juan Islands, *30*, *33*, *37*, *41*, *42*, *43*, *91*, *92*, *93*
Scripts
    Calling a marina, 136
    Calling a ship, *138*
    Calling another vessel, *146*
    Calling Coast Guard, *143*, *293*
    Calling Vessel Traffic, *142*
    Lingo, marine radio, *141*
    MAYDAY, *133*
    PON PON, 134
    Securite, *135*

SE Alaska. *See Southeast Alaska*
Septic System, *169*
South Puget Sound, *38*
Southeast Alaska, *38*, *54*, *56*, *57*, *192*, *229*
Suncor Stainless Steel 360 Degree Anchor Swivel, *170*
Sunshine Coast, *33*, *37*, *45*, *46*, *91*, *93*

T

Telephones, *148*
Tethers, 118
The Burgee, *39*, *41*, *43*, *44*, *93*, *138*, *243*, *270*
Tides, *208*
Tools, *172*
    Boat Systems, *175*
    House, *173*
Traps, crab and prawn, *231*
Trash. *See* Garbage
Trip Hazards, *117*
Tsunamis, *229*

U

Urban vs. Wilderness Cruising. *See* Wilderness vs. Urban Cruising

V

Vancouver, *8*, *31*, *41*, *43*, *44*, *45*, *46*, *47*, *51*, *52*, *91*, *92*, *93*, *116*, *129*, *130*, *183*, *200*, *210*, *242*, *248*, *285*
VHF radios and channels, *86*, *128*, *129*, *130*, *131*, *136*, *285*, *286*

W

Waggoner Cruising Guide, *29, 31, 32, 35, 36, 37, 39, 40, 42, 44, 46, 48, 50, 52, 53, 54, 55, 65, 69, 91, 95, 130, 131, 136, 138, 154, 155, 183, 184, 192, 211, 212, 215, 226, 236, 239, 240, 241, 243, 248, 255, 257, 270*

Wakes, *233*
Water, *116*
   Drinking, *116*
Weather, *245*
   Buoys, location of, *248*
   Collecting data, *246*
   Information provided, *249*
   Lighthouses, *248*
Whistles, *76, 82*

Joanne Wilshin

Made in United States
Troutdale, OR
01/11/2024